SUCCESS

THEY DID IT THE ACE ACADEMY WAY!

SECRETS FROM 26 LDS FILIPINOS

WITH INSPIRING RULES OF THUMB

ACADEMY FOR
CREATING ENTERPRISE
STOPRMPOVERTY.ORG

Editor: Kellene Ricks Adams
Cover and interior design: Stephen Carter
Publishing services: Christopher Bigelow, Scrivener Books

Published by:
Academy for Creating Enterprise
2520 N. University Ave #100
Provo, UT 84604 USA
(801) 735-1860
stopRMpoverty.org

ISBN 978-1-949165-07-4

This book is dedicated to the more than 400 families who have continued to follow the admonition of King Benjamin and shared their substance with 16,000 Academy students since the Academy was established on November 6, 1999, in Cebu, the Philippines.

ACE ACADEMY RULES OF THUMB

1. Sell What the Market Will Buy
2. Practice Separate Entities
3. Start Small, Think Big
4. Be Nice Later
5. Keep Good Records
6. Pay Yourself a Livable Salary
7. Buy Low, Sell High
8. Don't Eat Your Inventory
9. Use Multiple Suppliers
10. Buy on Credit, Sell for Cash
11. Purchase in Bulk
12. Use Suggestive Selling
13. Increase Sales, Decrease Costs
14. Turn Your Inventory Often
15. Value Your Customers
16. Differentiate Your Business
17. Hire Slow, Fire Fast
18. Inspect More, Assume Less
19. Have Written Agreements
20. Work on Your Business Ten Hours a Day, Five and a Half Days a Week
21. Practice Kaizen
22. Make a Profit Every Day
23. Work on Your Business, Not Just in Your Business
24. Write Down Daily and Weekly Business Goals
25. Focus, Focus, Focus

Plus:

Integrity before Profit
Delayed Gratification

CONTENTS

STEPHEN W. AND BETTE GIBSON
FOUNDERS, THE ACE ACADEMY

Introduction

Happy 20th Anniversary!

This year—2019—marks 20 years that the Academy for Creating Enterprise (the ACE Academy) has been helping people. And not just helping people but teaching them time-tested and proven business ideals and principles that, when followed, have transformed their lives as they've started their own businesses.

Our curriculum has been recognized by other leading nonprofit organizations that have reached out, asking if they too could adopt these lessons. The Church of Jesus Christ of Latter-day Saints even incorporated ACE training into much of its Starting and Growing My Business program.

We've been called the "MTC of Temporal Success" as our approach to creating business owners has reflected the Prophet Joseph Smith's counsel to "teach them correct principles, and they govern themselves." In fact, our focus on teaching self-reliance rather than simply providing relief has proven over and over again—thousands upon thousands of times—to create individuals who are confident, creative, kind, and unselfish.

But the ACE Academy is about so much more than simply teaching basic business practices. While what our students learn in the classroom are, indeed, golden nuggets of business wisdom, it is the graduates themselves who are the most valuable commodity we produce.

In the past two decades, more than 16,000 people in the Philippines, Mexico, Peru, and elsewhere have learned about our rules of thumb and gained other invaluable insights into being a successful entrepreneur. The ACE graduates profiled in this anniversary keepsake book offer only a glimpse of the thousands of individuals who have found security and success by applying what is taught in our courses and reinforced in our more than 420 chapters worldwide.

The Wide Scope of Success

Choosing which graduates to profile in this book was difficult! We could have told many hundreds of similar stories of success and service. Some of these wonderful Saints experienced failure after failure before their education at the Academy provided the fundamentals that would bring hard-won success. We've chosen several husband/wife entrepreneurial teams because watching couples work side-by-side as they climb out of poverty and establish financial stability and success is particularly rewarding.

The influence of ACE reaches beyond our graduates. For example, the ACE-coached business operators profiled in this book have an estimated total of 500 employees on their payrolls, an average of 20 employees each. If you include the temporary employees who work for the two staffing companies among these profiles, the total number of employees tops 1,000, for an average of about 40 employees per business.

Let's not stop there! If each business owner or employee has a family averaging five members (small by Filipino standards), we're talking about more than 5,000 individuals who are fed and sheltered because someone learned about and followed ACE principles.

No wonder we hear over and over again that "attending the Academy was the best decision I ever made." The Academy is a force for righteousness and good in the world, dedicated to helping those we serve become a Zion people with "no poor among them" (Moses 7:18). We believe the Academy is a vehicle to help fulfill the Book of Mormon prophecy that as members keep the commandments, they will prosper in their land.

Starting in the Philippines

It's appropriate that these success profiles are from the Philippines, where Bette and I first began our ACE endeavors (future volumes will profile entrepreneurs from additional countries). Early on, Bette and I knew we wanted to become involved in an educational experience of some sort. I had learned that, out of 300,000 young adult members of The Church of Jesus Christ of Latter-day Saints who turn 18 every year, only 10,000 would be able to attend a

Church-owned school. We yearned to extend a BYU experience to more of these bright, faithful young adults who were eagerly seeking an education within the framework of faith. And we committed from day one to help them stay in their own country for their education and help build up the kingdom there.

We then discovered that more than 1 million members of the Church are underemployed, with returned missionaries in third-world countries especially needing assistance. (We must remember the Academy was started even before President Gordon B. Hinckley introduced the Perpetual Education Fund in April 2001.) As we continued to contemplate where we might best make a difference, we discovered that 68 percent of Church members in the Philippines—one of the areas with the most rapid Church growth—lived below official poverty levels; this level was substantially higher than the already staggering national poverty rate of 49 percent. When we learned that more Church members live in the Philippines than in any other country in the world other than the United States, Mexico, and Brazil, we knew we had found our starting spot.

Our experience in the Philippines has been sweet, tender, and incredibly fulfilling. We have been blessed to expand our efforts to more countries, offering an increasing number of enthusiastic entrepreneurs the opportunity to build growing businesses on solid foundations. With the help of so many others, the Academy has created something of value that lasts and multiplies. In fact, when we mentioned in 1999 our idea to Elder Henry B. Eyring about starting an academy to teach returned missionaries, he said those very words: "Create something that lasts and multiplies." We have tried to do that.

Our Thanks and Invitation

On this milestone anniversary, we thank all those who have played critical roles in the growth and development of the Academy for Creating Enterprise. We cannot begin to name everyone, but our hearts are full as we look back on the many who have joined with us in an effort to not just give men and women "fish" but to teach them to "fish" and then **teach them how to sell their "fish" to others for a profit.**

We also invite anyone and everyone to join us in our efforts. You will find many ways to become involved, such as donating money to help make ACE self-reliant or donating time in support of local ACE chapters. We have nearly 200 chapters just in the Philippines and more than 420 worldwide. In a given month, more than 6,500 members meet in these chapters to celebrate their successes, learn, and mentor one another.

And finally, if you are facing poverty and can feel the spark of entrepreneurship growing within your own mind or heart, we invite you to join the many ACE students who have discovered how applying an ACE education can help them change their lives. Sign up for a training or join a chapter, and find out for yourself why our unofficial slogan has become: "My dream is not to die in poverty but to have poverty die in me."

—STEPHEN W. AND BETTE GIBSON
STOPRMPOVERTY.ORG

WORLDWIDE SCOPE OF THE ACE ACADEMY
Brazil (established 2019), Mexico (2010)
Peru (2013), Philippines (1999), Venezuela (2018)

Breaking the Chains of Poverty

Filipinos are often referred to as one of the happiest peoples on earth! For example, according to a United Nations report, the Philippines is ranked as the third happiest country in Asia. If asked what the reasons are for Filipinos' happiness, I believe the common answers would be—and interestingly they all start with the letter F—family, faith, and freedom.

But there's one component that many Filipinos do not enjoy, and that is financial stability. Many Filipinos suffer in silence from not being able to eat three times a day. Many experience bad living conditions. These difficulties, though, have taught Filipinos the value of hard work and perseverance, although most often this hard work lacks the proper guidance needed to get the desired financial rewards.

When I first heard Stephen W. and Bette Gibson's Business Rules of Thumb taught in the Academy some twenty years ago, I said to myself: "This is the missing piece to the Filipinos' financial stability puzzle!" Many Filipinos don't need another lesson or even motivation on working hard, but we can definitely use a lot of guidance on how and where to focus our muscles. A 200-watt light bulb can nicely light up a room, but a 200-watt laser can cut through steel!

This book is a testament of the combined power of hard work and correct principles. The stories repeatedly teach us that following correct business principles will yield business success. It's not a matter of IF but WHEN. Combining two atoms of hydrogen and one atom of oxygen will create water not sometime, not most of the time, but all the time!

These stories teach us that the hindrance to growth and success is not the lack of resources but the lack of resourcefulness, not limited money but a limiting mindset. It's not about living in a third-world country but about keeping a third-class mentality! The stories in this book will inspire readers to break the chains of poverty.

I am grateful to have been part of the Academy for 16 years now. My wife and I have seen wonderful changes in the lives of faithful Filipino Saints because they have learned powerful lessons from Steve and Bette, from the Academy staff, and from many dedicated Filipino church leaders who all preach one common self-reliance message: teach the Filipinos how to fish, and they will have fish for the rest of their lives!

Kudos to all our Academy alumni who carved their own definition of success through entrepreneurship. We are all proud of you, of what you've become and what good you are doing for others. Here's to more years of entrepreneurial success for you and the generations to come!

—James and Cynthia Fantone
ACE Philippines Country Manager and Office Manager

ACE Executive and Board Members

Executive Members
G. Andrew Barfuss
H. Lewis Swain
Norman Wright
Diane Nelson
Robert Harbertson
Stephen W. Gibson

Board Members
Steven J. Andersen
G. Andrew Barfuss
Roger Beattie
Jordan Clements
Ryan Freeman
Martin Frey
Bette Gibson
Stephen W. Gibson
Robert Harbertson
Ned Hill
Doug Holmes
Robb Jones
Leslie Layton
Steven Meek
Diane Nelson
Nancy Smith
H. Lewis Swain
Paul Warner
Norman Wright

Chief Executive Officer
Robert Heyn

Chief Impact Officer
Kim Gibson

Rufino and Tess **MEJIA**

Applied Entrepreneurship Training, 2013

"Better Than a Four-year Degree"

ICE CANDY MANUFACTURING AND DISTRIBUTION

Ask for an ice candy (frozen juice in a plastic tube) in Northern Philippines, and you'll receive a brightly wrapped treat labelled Frostville Ice Candy. The pink letters against a blue background are instantly recognizable to the locals,

Tarlac
●

and children even collect the logo stickers. In fact, in Gerona, Frostville is what you say to the vendor when asking for an ice candy; the brand has become synonymous with the beloved Filipino treat—a treat made sweeter and better by Rufino and Teresa Mejia.

The idea behind the brand name—which is catchy and easy for buyers to remember—comes from a Facebook game called Farmville, which the Mejias enjoyed playing. The similarity between their business and the game, explains Rufino, is that in Farmville, players earn pretend money by harvesting digital crops, while in Frostville, the Mejias earn real money by mixing, packing, and freezing ice candy.

The Mejias' sweet success actually began with financial hardship and rejection. Both husband and wife worked for a family member who owned a loan and microfinance business. Unfortunately, the business wasn't doing well, and people had to be laid off. Rufino volunteered to "retire" so that others could keep their jobs.

But he couldn't afford to not work. He considered looking for another job, but starting a family-owned business felt like the best option. The Mejias had always been intrigued by the idea of having their own business; they had even taken business training offered by the Academy in 2013. So they decided now was the time.

When Rufino and Teresa considered possible products to sell, the first thing that came into their minds was ice candy. The familiar treat was always a bestseller, especially in the heat of the summer. Initially, they wanted to own the franchise of an existing brand, but the franchise fees were expensive, the parent company provided little support to its franchise owners, and the Mejias didn't live within the metropolitan area where the company was based. They were disappointed when their franchise plan fell apart—although in the long run, the failure was a blessing in disguise.

Favorite Rules of Thumb

- Practice Kaizen
- Start Small, Think Big
- Value Your Customers

Undeterred, they decided to start their own ice candy business. They measured and mixed ingredients, poured the mixture into plastic packages, knotted each tube, then placed each treat into a freezer. The work was slow and tedious, but if it meant that they could somehow become financially stable, they would push forward.

One thing that differentiated Frostville from similar ice candy is the special powdered mix the Mejias used to make their product. Using a mix instead of raw ingredients reduces the cost of materials, plus it gives the ice candy a smoother texture, even when frozen. They knew they had a winning product when, after eating an early Frostville sample, their young niece yelled, "It's ice cream!" Teresa tried to explain that it wasn't actually ice cream, but the youngster insisted—and she isn't the only one who thinks Frostville treats taste special.

The ice treats quickly became popular, and the family worked hard to meet demand, but they could only make 500 products a day. Rufino's favorite rule of thumb from the Academy was **Practice Kaizen,** so the two were always looking for ways to improve working practices and personal efficiency. "We worried less about capital and money," Rufino says, "and focused on improvement, results, and performance."

A breakthrough for Frostville came when an aunt lent them money to buy a mixing machine. This meant they no longer needed to produce everything by hand; the machine would mix and seal the ice candy into the plastic wraps—a method that was not only faster but also more hygienic. Eventually, the couple purchased four more machines, and today Frostville produces 50,000 iced candies a day, and has grown to include sellers and distributors on two other large islands.

The road to success hasn't always been easy. In fact, Rufino notes that "failures are life's tuition fee." But the Mejias have relied heavily on the training they received at the Academy and credit that training for much of their growth and success. "At the Academy, we learned how to stay motivated and how to wisely invest our time, money, energy, and effort into our business," Teresa says. "To us, the Academy is better than a four-year degree."

Today, many children—and adults—in Tarlac and other places in the Philippines enjoy the unique blend of

"We worried less about capital and money, and focused on improvement, results, and performance."

Frostville ice candy. Stickers that carry the logo designed by their own son are carefully removed from the plastic as Frostville fans work to complete their collection; after all, there are "only" eighteen flavors to choose from.

But Frostville is about more than cool refreshment and sticker collections. The Mejias have been able to put all four children through college, enjoy a comfortable lifestyle, and provide employment and partnership opportunities for others.

"Frostville is heaven sent!" the Mejias often say, as they consider their long journey from franchise heartbreak to selling their wares in the local market to becoming a leading brand in their area and beyond. As they supply schools, supermarkets, and stores with tens of thousands of delightful Frostville treats, they are eternally grateful for the blessings they have enjoyed through owning their own business.

Dino and Flordeliza **AGULAN**

Applied Entrepreneurship Training, 2008

Dreaming of Bigger Things

FURNITURE MAKING

When he was a young married man almost two decades ago, Dino Agulan's commute to work entailed walking outside his back door into his back yard. His job? Supplying and resizing wood for local furniture makers.

But although Dino worked hard, his family struggled to make ends meet. As he worked on each piece of wood, Dino dreamed of bigger things. "I'll give you hundreds, then thousands of pesos," he promised his wife, Flordeliza.

Lingayen

"And someday, millions!"

And although he truly believed it, he wasn't sure how he could make it happen.

Until one day when a customer of his who made furniture came to his home to pick up a load of wood—in a newly purchased truck. *If this customer could afford to purchase a truck,* thought Dino, *maybe instead of just cutting wood, I could make furniture.* The path to increasing his family's income had now become clear.

Dino took the idea and ran with it. He combined his wood supply and expertise with what little the family had been able to save and hired a single employee, a skilled furniture maker. The risk paid off in a big way: the next month he had enough work—and income—to hire three additional workers.

That was in 1999, and Dino has never looked back. By 2001, the Agulans had eight workers, and in 2003, they signed a contract with a sawmill in La Union to buy scrap lumber, formally registered their business name—Flordin Furniture—and rented a nearby space to use as their warehouse and office. Dino had left his backyard wood-cutting behind.

Running the business didn't come easily, and Dino and Flordeliza faced many challenges as they worked together to grow and develop their company. Attending the Onsite Training Program at the Academy was a huge turning point for them. "If we had not attended ACE, there would be no place to sit here!" says Dino, as he points to the well-made chairs, sofas, and table in the living room of his home—all furniture from his company.

At the Academy, the Agulans learned invaluable business practices, including **Practice Separate Entities,** approaching business with a systematic outlook, and the power of delegation. And delegation has become essential as they have continued to grow. In 2017, the couple

Favorite Rules of Thumb

- Value Your Customers
- Practice Separate Entities

DINO AND FLORDELIZA AGULAN

started a second company: My Home Decor Furniture.

Originally, Flordin Furniture resized wood and made cabinets and cupboards; eventually the Agulans added solid furniture to their product line. Today, the two companies operate as wholesale and retail furniture manufacturers that supply furniture to two branch locations and seven mall stores in Pangasinan, as well as custom-made orders for individual buyers. They have 32 employees, including several trained furniture makers.

Dino runs Flordin Furniture while Flordeliza handles My Home Decor. But they work side by side, con-

stantly learning from and supporting each other as they strive to be a little more hands-off with the business and more focused on raising their daughter and three sons. The two focus on the management and finance sides of their businesses, including personally addressing any customer concerns about products, a practice that makes them stand out among local furniture businesses and a principle—**Value Your Customers**—they learned at the Academy. And because they have created a reputation of excellent craftsmanship and trustworthiness, both their wholesale and retail businesses are succeeding.

They work side by side, constantly learning from and supporting each other.

Dino often reflects on the vow he made to his wife long ago when he was working in their backyard. Through hard work, dedication, and the application of sound business principles, he's kept that promise. And he's not done—the two are planning on adding more branch locations and have started a new business, opening a restaurant near their new house. "We are so grateful and are definitely enjoying our blessings," Dino says.

Belsie and Lilibeth **AGUSTIN**

Onsite Training Training, 2012
Applied Entrepreneurship Training, 2015
ACE My Business Training, 2016

Failing Forward

MEDIA/BILLBOARD SERVICES

When Belsie Agustin started his first business—a coin-operated video game that charged one peso for five minutes of play—a friend gave him a *25 Business Rules of Thumb* pamphlet, distributed by the ACE Academy. Although his business failed, Belsie studied the contents of the pamphlet, referring to it as his business bible as he contemplated future business opportunities.

Zamboanga

By following the sound business principles that he learned from the Academy pamphlet years before he actually attended classes, Belsie has "failed forward," learning from every step and mistake along the way. "If not," he asks, "what can be learned?"

One of the things he learned is not to rush into starting his own business. In fact, he first had the idea of building billboards in his hometown of Zamboanga in 1999, but it wasn't until 2004 that he signed his first client. Those five years were spent envisioning how he was going to run his advertising company and finding necessary starting capital. During those lean planning years, he worked a full-time government job and searched for business partners.

Once his first client—Bobson Jeans—signed on the dotted line, Belsie was off and running, creating his first billboards. Two friends agreed to provide backing, and Belsie launched Alberei Advertising Corporation (the name is an acronym created from the first names of Belsie and his partners). Within a few years, Alberei's billboards were proudly serving some of the area's biggest names, including Sun Cellular, Globe, Cebu Pacific, and many more.

That doesn't mean that everything went smoothly. But when Belsie started Alberei, he had determined to apply everything he'd learned from his "bible" and the Academy, so he and his wife, Lilibeth, persevered even when things looked bleak.

As a minor entity in the media industry, Alberei struggled to grow its clientele. At one point, Belsie was thrilled when Sun Cellular, a major telecommunications company, was about to sign a contract—only to cancel in the end because, they said, Alberei was still a small player in the industry. Belsie and Lilibeth admit to being discouraged, but Belsie likens business to a crocodile, which doesn't just snap the moment it sees its prey but waits patiently

Favorite Rules of Thumb

- Buy Low, Sell High
- Practice Separate Entities

for the right moment to strike. Of course, clients aren't prey, Belsie says, but waiting patiently while planning is definitely essential to success.

Shortly after Sun Cellular backed out, one of the area's largest real estate companies, Filinvest, signed a five-year contract. Before long, Sun Cellular was back as well. Belsie invested the profits back into the company and constructed more sites for advertising placements, and business boomed. Belsie's patience had paid off.

Eventually the Agustins actually attended three of the Academy's programs, starting with the Onsite Training Program in 2012 and followed by the Applied Entrepreneurship Program in 2015 and the ACE My Business Program in 2016. The couple learned even more important business principles—including **Practice Separate Entities** and **Buy Low, Sell High**—that continued to guide them as the business grew and expanded. Thanks to the Academy, the couple realized they were more than ready to continue to chase their dreams.

So Belsie seized the opportunity to grow, expanding beyond simply providing quality advertising to tapping the power of media to bring services and information to the people. He added a radio station and TV channel to his portfolio, calling these two ventures EMedia Productions. The radio station tops the FM waves and provides local news and traffic updates in the local dialect, Chabacano; the TV station is also a growing network.

And Lilibeth is currently running her dream business—a laundry shop—with Belsie providing invaluable support, coaching, and mentoring to help her avoid the common mistakes that many new business owners make. He also serves as a sounding board, with the couple discussing concerns and challenges as she tackles the daily grind of operating her shop. In addition,

Patience has paid off for him in the past, and Belsie is confident it will continue to pay off moving forward.

Belsie serves as a Starting and Growing My Business instructor for the Church's self-reliance program.

Although the Agustins are eyeing possible expansion into the islands of Visayas, Luzon, and Mindanoa, Belsie is proud to keep Alberei and its sister media companies centered in Zamboanga because, he says, "local is king!" True to this statement, Alberei has built more than 40 billboards scattered throughout Zamboanga, with the largest project being the giant Jollibee bucket billboard representing the fast-food chain's bestselling fried chicken bucket.

Today Belsie is a majority owner of Alberei, which currently enjoys 90 percent market share of the billboard business in Zamboanga. In addition to EMedia, he is also involved in several sister companies, including Frostville, Inc. (an ice candy producer); Goldstone, Inc. (agricultural manpower); and Philtech, Inc. (a payment systems facility). He and Lilibeth also plan on serving short-term temple missions when their 10-year-old daughter, Nicole, starts college. But Belsie isn't rushing into anything. Much like his entry into advertising, he is taking it slow and careful. After all, patience has paid off for him in the past, and Belsie is confident it will continue to pay off moving forward.

Sheila Capito Estrada **GRANADA**

Applied Entrepreneurship Training, 2013
ACE My Business Training, 2013

"Now I Can Clearly See"
OPTOMETRIST

She'd been a business owner for almost 20 years, but she recognized the power of an ACE Academy training—and jumped at the chance to attend when it was offered to her.

Sheila Capito Estrada Granada had owned her optometrist clinic in Candon for almost two decades, but the journey had not been easy. In fact, when she signed up for the Academy's intensive business training in 2013, she felt desperate and hopeless, as if the problems she was facing as a business owner were insurmountable.

A licensed optometrist—she graduated in 1994 from Lyceum Northwestern University—Sheila had started the business in 1995 so she could enjoy flexibility and freedom while raising her family, which now includes three grown children and a granddaughter. Her husband, Mario, who was also an optometrist, worked abroad for years to provide a stable income while the business grew.

Sheila poured her heart and soul into the business. In addition to being the doctor, she managed the day-to-day operations, functioning as secretary, assistant, accountant, and even bill collector. Despite her best efforts, her business floundered prior to her Academy training.

Candon

In 2009, she and Mario decided that being apart was too dif-

> Learn your craft,
> master your roles,
> and work harder
> than everyone else.

ficult and their family needed to be a priority. Mario moved home, and the two worked side by side to make the business grow. They managed to survive on the meager income the clinic produced, but when Sheila had a chance to sign up for the Academy's four-week intensive entrepreneurial training, she didn't hesitate.

The program is based on a set of business principles called the rules of thumb, and Sheila knew if she paid attention, she could transform the struggling clinic into a profitable business. "I enrolled and, like a sponge, absorbed as much knowledge as I could," says Sheila, who points to the **Keep Good Daily Records** lesson as a defining moment.

"I learned to write down every transaction that happens in my business," she continues, "so that at the end of the day I know what our income was for every day and where the last 25 centavos was spent." Sheila keeps notebooks and notebooks of records, and she now understands how this daily practice can make her an expert in spotting problems by just merely looking at her logbooks.

Sheila is a living example of another Academy principle: never give up. She instinctively understood that lesson, but she gained insight into its importance through her Academy training. "Everyone who is involved in business knows how difficult the road is," she notes. "But there is no shortcut to success. You can't say you want to be succesful but then do nothing. Learn your craft, master your roles, and work harder than everyone else."

Today, Sheila's hard work has paid off. Her clinic has grown to six branches with 10 employees, and each of her children are involved in the family business and pursuing degrees in optometry as well. And she hasn't stopped there. Sheila has taken two more Academy courses, and the family business now includes a laundry shop, a salon, and a travel and tourism office, with 12 more employees helping run these ventures.

Sheila calls her employees the X factor of her success, and another

Favorite Rules of Thumb

- Keep Good Daily Records
- Hire Slow, Fire Fast

Academy lesson she takes to heart is to **Hire Slow, Fire Fast**. "I love to hire friends and church mates," she observes. "But I make it clear from the beginning what their roles and responsibilities are, which should be strictly complied with to avoid termination. I have fired many, but I've retained a lot.

"It has always been a policy of mine to give what is due to my employees," she continues. "I know in my heart that when I take care of my people, my people will take care of my businesses."

After more than 20 years, Sheila is enjoying the flexibility and freedom she was looking for when she first started her business. "Once I learned how to run the business properly, I found time to spend with my children and husband," she says. "I have learned to balance my tasks at work, at church, and at home. Thanks to what I learned at the Academy, I can clearly see how to succeed, help others, and enjoy my life."

Francisco and Melca **BAUTISTA**

Applied Entrepreneurship Training, 2015

Developing Step by Step

HOME BUILDER

When Francisco Bautista was young, the bank foreclosed on his family's home. Devastated, the young boy promised himself that someday he would never have to worry about his home being taken from him again.

As he grew up, his dream grew even broader: he set his sights on becoming a property developer so that he

Montatban

could build or buy homes, then sell them, creating a legacy of providing others with an opportunity to own their own homes.

As he became more familiar with what it would take to turn his dream into reality, Francisco identified the road he needed to take to achieve that goal, and in 2009 he and his wife, Melca, became real estate agents, taking the first step on that road.

Francisco and Melca knew that building a business in the real estate world was tough, competitive—and expensive. But they were undeterred. Saving every penny, they worked toward the next step, which was achieved in 2011 when Francisco became an official real estate broker. Two more years of careful budgeting and hard work, and the Bautistas opened Great Empire Realty, their own real estate brokerage.

But that wasn't the end of their journey. They were getting close to the goal Francisco had identified years earlier of becoming a developer—a goal that would give them more control over the business aspect of their lives and allow them to provide input on their projects as well as enjoy financial independence. In 2015, the Bautistas began their first build-and-sell project, a two-story, Japanese-inspired house. They had become developers—Francisco had fulfilled the promise he'd made to his parents.

As the couple took their steps toward becoming developers, they had realized that money wasn't the only issue. In addition to funding, they knew they needed business training. Although they'd worked as real estate agents and in a real estate brokerage, they recognized that running brokerage and development companies was a vastly different experience.

With that in mind, the same year they bought their first development project, both Francisco and Melca attended the Applied Entrepreneurship Program offered by the Academy. From the training, they learned

Favorite Rules of Thumb

- Buy Low, Sell High
- Don't Eat Your Inventory

> Becoming developers means much more than simply selling a house.

two important concepts: **Buy Low, Sell High** and **Don't Eat Your Inventory**. They also learned tips to keep their capital intact, since they knew they needed money to invest in the properties they planned to develop and sell. And they learned to create a manageable business system that would allow them to manage and delegate to employees.

It's worth noting that the Bautistas attended Academy training while in the middle of their first project. "ACE was timely," says Francisco. "What we learned helped us catch the things we might have been doing incorrectly and improve these things while we still could. If we hadn't made these changes, it may have been costly for us in the long run."

In addition, the couple noted, by the time they made their first sale as independent brokers, they had learned the art of negotiation and were equipped to make wiser decisions. And they continue to use these invaluable Academy lessons as they pursue additional development projects.

Recognizing the difference their Academy training has made in their business lives, the Bautistas eagerly share the Academy lessons they've learned with fellow real estate agents, as well as their employees, friends, and family members. Their favorite lessons to share are the ones related to savings, spending wisely, and finding the entrepreneur inside of you.

For the Bautistas, becoming developers means much more than simply selling a house; they are creating homes.

Julius and Marissa **CAILER**

Applied Entrepreneurship Training, 2009

Wired for Success

HARDWARE STORE

The birth of a child can be an impetus for change in many ways. For registered master electrician Julius Cailer, the arrival of his new daughter motivated him to reevaluate what he wanted out of life.

Julius worked full-time with an electrical company,

specializing in house wiring. He enjoyed what he did, but when he and his wife, Marissa, took a hard look at the future of their family, they decided they wanted more than just a job—they set their sights on increased financial security, flexibility, and fulfillment.

Those things would come, they decided, if they could become business owners.

In 2009, they started a side business. A friend had showed them how to make their own floor wax, so they invested ₱20,000 in their own floor-wax-making company. Within six months, they were in trouble: they were buying the materials to make their floor wax with cash, but their customers were buying the final product on credit. That was a setback when it came to income as the operation quickly became strapped for cash.

Cauyan

About this same time, the Cailers attended the Academy's Applied Entrepreneurship Program. Thanks to this train-

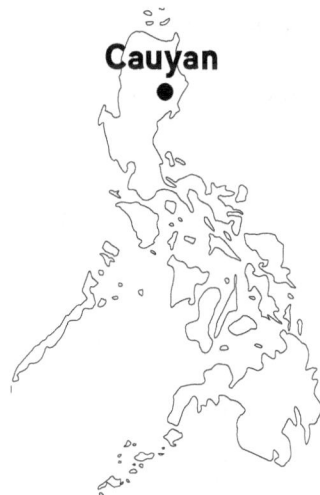

> Today, a valued group of electrician clients consistently purchases at least 70 percent of their electrical wiring supplies from Julius.

ing, they were able to recognize which business habits they needed to change and how to make corrections to get their business on the right path. For example, they learned to **Buy on Credit, Sell for Cash,** instead of the other way around. They discovered the principle of **Start Small, Think Big**. And they made sure to **Practice Separate Entities** and **Pay Yourself a Livable Salary**.

By following these good business habits, their business began to grow, and they looked for other products to offer. Because of Julius's background and expertise as an electrician, it was natural for them to expand in that direction. One thing electricians always need is electrical wire, so the couple started there, initially selling on a small scale until they realized they could make a better profit if they followed another Academy rule of thumb: **Purchase in Bulk**. They found a supplier, spread the word to Julius's friends and colleagues, and today they have a valued group of electrician clients who consistently purchase at least 70 percent of their electrical wiring supplies from Julius.

But that was just the beginning. In 2012, they began selling plumbing supplies and moved into their first shop, calling the business Jehan Leigh Electrical Supplier and General Merchandise. By using the word *general*, the Cailers keep their options open and are always looking for new products to add to their inventory. Sure enough, in 2017 they began supplying general hardware items and hollow blocks.

Value Your Customers—another Academy principle—is a high priority for Julius and Marissa. They stay in close contact with their regular customers, anticipating needs and addressing any concerns and questions. They hand

Favorite Rules of Thumb

- Buy on Credit, Sell for Cash
- Start Small, Think Big
- Practice Separate Entities
- Pay Yourself a Livable Salary
- Value Your Customers

out Christmas gifts and invite their customers to the company's annual Christmas party.

Through the years, they've also learned to delegate, hiring additional people to assist them; today Jehan Leigh Electrical Supplier and General Merchandise has eight employees on its payroll.

Following these tried-and-true business practices will help the Cailers achieve the goals they are working toward. Julius plans on officially retiring from his full-time job in the next five years, allowing him to focus solely on the business. He and Marissa are confident that their business, which also provides employ-

ment to their extended family, will be able to provide comfortably for their needs. In addition to the financial stability they will enjoy, they are also excited about having even more time to fulfill their Church callings and serve the Lord in whatever capacity He asks.

Truly, the Cailers have found more than just a job as they have grown their own business. Their patience and hard work have brought them the financial security, flexibility, and fulfillment that once they had only dreamed of.

Deimler Ogas and Perlie **CUYAN**

Residential Executive Training, 2011
Applied Entrepreneurship Training, 2013

An Empire in the Making

TAXI, GAS STATION, AND GROCERY STORE

A mother's love and commitment can change a son's life forever—especially when her priorities become his.

In Deimler Ogas Cuyan's third year of college, his mother applied for a loan to pay for his college tuition. The family was hardworking, but money was tight. And a college education was worth going into debt for, said Deimler's mother. She was devastated when her loan application was rejected, and to this day—more than three decades later—Deimler remembers the look on his mother's face when she told him the news.

Somehow, the 19-year-old student managed to finish college, earning a degree in political science, and he served a mission for The Church of Jesus Christ of Latter-day Saints. But when he returned and started working, the memory of his mother's face lingered in the back of his mind. Initially, he worked for the government and then got involved in a buy-and-sell company, but eventually he decided to pursue his own business. Inspired by his tender memory, Deimler chose to go into microcredit, or lending small amounts of money at low interest to individuals working to become self-employed—and Doc & P Credit and Loan Service, Inc., was born.

Working in the field of lending, Deimler vowed to provide

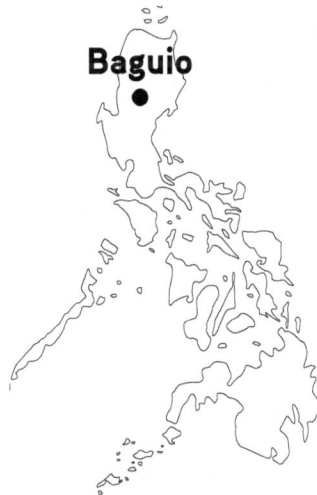

One thing has motivated every business venture Deimler has undertaken—his desire to help and serve others.

his clients with a positive loan experience, so he built a service-oriented microcredit company. He determined to ensure that his clients received the assistance they needed, including educating them about the financial responsibilities and benefits of taking out their loan.

After starting Doc & P, Deimler realized that running businesses was deeply rewarding in many ways, so he started three—yes, three—more businesses. He franchised a taxi service and purchased used taxis. He eventually added more vehicles to his fleet and then expanded to car rentals; today he has six taxis and nine rental cars.

His next move was natural, given his taxi and car-rental businesses; he looked into franchising a fueling station. However, after thinking it through, he decided instead to study the industry and build his own station. Today his Interland Oil Fuel Station is Deimler's highest-earning endeavor, grossing almost ₱4 million a month.

Next Deimler branched out into mini-grocery stores, or mini-marts. Initially, that wasn't what he had in mind when he was looking around Bataan for property to lease. But then he discovered a lot with an abandoned cinema. The price was affordable, and looking around, Deimler noticed that the area had no grocery stores. Blessed with an ability to see a need and then meet it, he immediately envisioned what would become DPC Caladio Mart. That venture was so successful that he opened a second mart in his own city, Baguio.

But how did Deimler manage to run all these businesses simultaneously—and so successfully? While he's definitely naturally inclined to recognize business opportunities, he credits his training in the Academy's Residential Executive Program in 2011 for much of his skill and expertise.

At the Academy, he learned to Keep Good Re-

Favorite Rules of Thumb

- Keep Good Records
- Work on Your Business, Not Just in Your Business
- Hire Slow, Fire Fast

cords and have a working system—both of which are critical to being able to **Work on Your Business, Not Just in Your Business**. And **Hire Slow, Fire Fast** ensures the quality of employees you hire. Operating your business—or businesses, in Deimler's case—while living the gospel of Jesus Christ and fulfilling Church callings (Deimler is a Sunday School teacher and ward employment specialist) brings a rich balance between temporal and spiritual that elevates both mind and heart.

While Deimler observes that he doesn't favor one business over another, one thing has motivated every business venture he's undertaken: his desire to help and serve others. His mother's memory continues to be a guiding force even today.

Junard and Leizel **LAYUGAN**

Applied Entrepreneurship Training, 2009

"More Than I Bargained For"

ADVERTISING SERVICES

Junard Layugan was working abroad as a caregiver when he signed up to attend the Applied Entrepreneurship Program at the Academy during a visit home in 2009 to see his family. Desperate to find a way to stay in the Philippines with his wife and four children, Junard found both

Cauayan

the training and confidence he needed to make that happen at the Academy. After completing the program, he took a leap of faith, deciding not to renew his caregiving contract in Israel and instead start his own business at home.

But what kind of a business should he start?

That choice became clear when he placed an order to have a tarpaulin canvas printed for a family event. When he picked up the tarpaulin—and found he didn't get what he had ordered—he knew he could do a better job. And Speed ACE Advertising was born.

With the blessing of his wife, Leizel, Junard took the family's precious savings and used it as capital to start the new business, investing in a tarpaulin-printing machine and renting a shop. The launch of business wasn't without challenges, as costs to operate the business totaled up faster than income generated by orders. But the big break came for Speed ACE when elections began and political candidates needed quality advertising materials, including tarpaulins.

Thanks to Junard and Leizel's hard work, Speed ACE outgrew its first location, and the Layugans found a better location for their business. But their journey to success was slowed by problems with budgeting and meeting deadlines. Junard refused to give up; he did not want to be separated from this wife and children ever again, not even for the biggest salary in the world. He determined to do whatever it took to make it in the Philippines.

Junard reviewed what he'd learned at the Academy, such as **Sell What the Market Will Buy** and **Increase Sales, Decrease Costs**, then looked for solutions and ways to improve. His hard work, perseverance, and the desire to provide quality advertising materials paid off. The family business now brings a gross monthly income

Favorite Rules of Thumb

- Start Small, Think Big
- Sell What the Market Will Buy
- Increase Sales, Decrease

He did not want to be separated from his wife and children ever again, not even for the biggest salary in the world.

of ₱2,000,000 and employs 18 people, each of whom the couple cherishes. Although Speed ACE started small, the Layugans thought big (another Academy principle), and now the company is one of the largest advertising service providers in the area. And with the success of one business under their belts, Junard and Leizel are now looking for new business ventures, including investing in real estate.

The Layugans will forever be grateful for the training Junard received from the Academy. In addition to the sound business practices he learned, Junard gained invaluable information about communication. He and Leizel have worked hard to develop open communication, and they refuse to let the challenges of running a business strain their marriage. In fact, Junard says, operating the business together has brought the two of them closer—not just geographically but also in the sense that he has learned to be present and focus on what truly matters.

"Truly I got more than I bargained for when I attended the Academy class," he concludes.

Pete **MAGUALE** Jr.

Residential Executive Training, 2008
ACE My Business Training, 2016

"I Found the Right Mentor"

PRINTING SERVICES

Pete Maguale Jr. and Roger Vegamora had known each other for years; they lived in the same district in Malaybalay and were close friends. But it wasn't until Pete attended the ACE Academy that he looked at Roger as a mentor.

Roger ran his own business—a printing shop—and he encouraged Pete to consider starting his own business as well. Being your own boss has incredible advantages, he told Pete. In fact, he even suggested Pete consider opening up his own printing shop. He wasn't worried about the competition; he just wanted his friend to succeed.

Pete is a communicator—and a talented one. His natural talent made him a great DJ on a local FM radio station in his hometown of Malaybalay City. He enjoyed playing a variety of music and chatting with listeners on the air, but he knew the pay wasn't enough to sustain his growing family long term. He knew he had to make a change.

When he heard about ACE Academy, he decided to sign up, hoping he'd find guidance and direction in pursuing a new career. He found exactly that—and so much more.

Malaybalay

One of the many valuable ideas the Academy teaches is the importance of a mentor. "Mentorship is encouraged because you can learn

Initially he started with a single computer and printer and catered primarily to the university students, but his end goal was much bigger.

directly from people with the same business ideas that you're considering," Pete says. "They can help you learn the ins and outs of the trade, teach you what to avoid, and guide you in the enterprise."

As Pete considered the suggestion, he realized it would be a perfect fit. At first glance, it might not seem like a printing station has much in common with being a DJ, but Pete realized that both require being friendly and outgoing, as well as an aptitude for communication. "You're just communicating messages in a different medium at a print shop than you are on the radio," Pete points out. "But when you stop and think about it, they are both crafts." So while Pete knew he would need a lot of mentoring in starting his brand-new business, he wouldn't be straying too far from his skill set.

In August 2010, Pete opened Print All Station, a print shop across the street from the town's university. Initially he started with a single computer and printer and catered primarily to the university students, but his end goal was much bigger: to become a go-to stop for everyone's print and design needs.

Although it took time and patience, Pete's business boomed under Roger's careful mentoring and by following the principles he'd learned at the Academy. He bought more computers and printers, he hired more employees, and he began printing more kinds of items. Today, the Print All Station really does print it all, from tarpaulin canvas signs and keychains to mugs, banners, and even logo-imprinted pens.

Pete can't stress enough the importance of finding a mentor and following the rules of thumb taught at the Academy. Without these, he says, "I may never have started my own business, which has brought me and my family so many blessings."

Favorite Rules of Thumb

- Make a Profit Every Day
- Practice Separate Entities
- Value Your Customers

Print All has expanded to three locations, has 30 employees, and has made it possible for Pete to support his own family. In fact, Pete's wife, Rosalie, was able to quit her teaching job and stay at home with the couple's three sons, a situation that would never have been possible if Pete had continued his stint as a radio DJ and not attended the Academy.

Pete may not be on the airwaves any more, but he is still reaching out—just in a different way.

Jess and Arlene **NORTIZA**

Applied Entrepreneurship Training, 2007 and 2011

Wheels of Fortune

TIRE DISTRIBUTORSHIPS

When Jess Nortiza first heard about the Academy's Residential Program, he recognized immediately the power the program could have to change his life.

Jess had grown up poor, and despite the fact that both he and his wife, Arlene, were working long hours, poverty

Valenzuela

was still part of their lives. Jess was determined to change that, he just didn't know exactly how.

Enter the Academy.

In 2009, Jess quit his job as a salesman for a tire-distribution company and attended the Academy's residential program. Before the program was over, he had a clear vision of what he needed to do to reach financial security. He bought a single fishball-vending cart and set out to achieve his dream of owning his own tire-distribution company.

"I started small with almost nothing," he says, "but I knew I had the capacity to grow."

In less than two years, his single fishball cart had grown to six, and Jess had saved enough money to take the next step: he bought gum paste and started patching broken tires for people in his community. In addition, he bought extra gum paste and became a wholesale distributor to vulcanizing shops in the area. His next step, he told Arlene, would be to buy his own vulcanizing shop and specialize in supplying and retailing wholesale tires for motorbikes, motorcycles, cars, and trucks. Wheels, he said, would be the key to their family's fortune.

Intrigued by Jess's enthusiasm and confidence for his new business—and admittedly a little nervous about their financial future—Arlene signed up for the Academy's Applied Entrepreneurship Program in 2011, hoping she could gain a glimpse into what was inspiring her husband. She understood almost immediately. "The knowledge I received from that class was an eye opener," she says. "I realized that simple people like us truly have the capacity to create a difference in our lives."

Arlene quit her job to join her husband in working for their future. She too had been working for a tire distribution company, in her case as an accounting clerk, so she focused her management and operation skills

Favorite Rules of Thumb

- Keep Good Records
- Pay Yourself a Livable Salary
- Start Small, Think Big
- Differentiate Your Business Costs

on running the company, which they had named Arje Trading, while Jess handled sales and marketing. Because the two had both attended Academy training, they were united in their efforts to follow sound business principles, especially **Keep Good Records**, **Pay Yourself a Livable Salary**, and **Start Small, Think Big**.

In addition to working to become financially secure themselves, Jess and Arlene also dreamed of helping others—particularly their extended family—achieve financial success. "We love to hire relatives," Jess observes. "We feel that we have an obligation to help them improve their lives because we know personally what poverty looks like. So initially we hired relatives left and right, and sure enough, we had headaches left and right as well."

Again, their Academy education paid off. This time they applied the lessons on systems creation as an effective solution. "We learned it the hard way, but we became better at screening employees, helping them understand company policies, and educating them about the consequences of noncompliance. I had to fire my own brother before I learned my lesson!" Jess lamented. The couple still prefers to hire relatives, but with proper hiring and training processes in place, they have fewer headaches and problems with their employees.

And their unselfishness extends even beyond hiring others. They often encourage others—even their own employees—to become entrepreneurs themselves. They've had more than one employee branch off and start similar businesses in their own hometowns. "One employee is now averaging ₱20,000 in sales, and he gets his supplies from us," Jess notes.

The Nortizas believe that anybody can create a business, but the chal-

> "I realized that simple people like us truly have the capacity to create a difference in our lives."

lenge is creating a business that lasts and stands out from the rest. **Differentiate Your Business**," notes Jess, emphasizing his Academy training. "Don't follow the competition. Intead, offer something better and innovative."

What makes the Nortizas' business stand out is the relationships they have created with their customers. "I make them laugh and provide headache-free services," Jess says. "We offer door-to-door delivery and follow a strict always-on-time policy. That is our promise to our customers." In fact, Jess actually encourages his customers to give the competition a try. "When they do," he notes, "they see for themselves the difference in quality of goods and services."

With their focus on solid business principles, Jess and Arlene have not forgotten to also focus on the Lord. Their success, they are quick to point out, is often rooted in the prayers they offer. "When we started the business, our prayers became specific," Arlene says."One time during a delivery, our truck stopped in the middle of the highway. After saying a prayer, we both knew who to call specifically to help us.

"We know we could not do much if we don't depend on God for guidance," she continues. "He answers specific

pleadings, and we have witnessed His love for us as we grow not only our family but also this business."

And the business *has* grown. Now called Jelyn Trading (and still a supplier and retailer of tires), their business does ₱8 million in monthly sales, has hired 22 full-time employees, and distributes tires in five different cities (Bi-col, Mindoro, Laoag, Zambales, and Leyte), with plans to expand to two more. "Capital is never the problem," says Jess, again relying on Academy business principles that have transformed his life. "And attitude is always the solution."

Thanks to the Academy, Jess and Arlene's attitude has definitely been the solution to their financial problems.

Rogelio and Adelina
VEGAMORA

Residential Executive Training, 2010

"We Put It All on the Line"

PRINTING SUPPLY BUSINESS

In August 2008, Roger and Adelina Vegamora took a leap of faith: they sold their house and invested the profits in a new business.

Through the years, Roger had tried his hand at several different ventures, failing every time. This time, however, both he and Adelina had finished the executive training at the ACE Academy, and they felt prepared and confident as they launched their print shop—so confident, in fact, that they were willing to risk their home.

So the Vegamoras moved into an apartment with their young children, purchased basic printing supplies such as tarpaulins, stickers, and posters, then got to work. "We had to succeed," says Roger. "We had invested everything we had—even our home—and this had to pay off so my family could eat."

Thankfully, it did. Within four years, not only had V8 Digital Solutions become a stable source of income for the Vegamoras, but the business had expanded from being a simple print shop to becoming a printing-supplies business when their own supplier offered them an opportunity to become a distributor. A few years later, the couple actually sold the printing segment of V8 Digital Solutions and focused solely on distributing printing supplies, expanding to include a second distributorship in Cagayan de Oro.

None of that would have been possible without the Academy program. "We learned many invaluable business principles, but for me, the most beneficial Academy lessons were **Practice Separate Entities**, **Pay Yourself a Livable Salary**, and **Integrity before Profit**," Roger says. "This training helped us manage our money wisely and attract more customers, who learned quickly that we were honest, offered quality products, and did quality work."

Other important Academy lessons include staying current with the latest business trends in their

Favorite Rules of Thumb

- Practice Separate Entities
- Pay Yourself a Livable Salary
- Integrity before Profit
- Delay Gratification

A milestone payoff day for the couple and their six children was signing on the dotted line to again purchase their own home.

industry, saving cash on hand, and understanding the importance of delayed gratification. "We learned that sacrificing a little now would pay off significantly later on," says Adelina.

Today, Roger is passionate about passing on his valuable knowledge to others. "We cannot be successful without a successor," he explains. His two oldest children work alongside him and Adelina in the business, and he has trained and guided other aspiring entrepreneurs, including a close friend who also runs a successful printing shop. Roger doesn't look at his friend's success as competition; rather, seeing others succeed makes him more grateful for the success he and his family have enjoyed.

Today, the Vegamora family no longer lives in a rented apartment. Their leap of faith paid off in many ways, but certainly a milestone payoff day for the couple and their six children was when they signed on the dotted line and to again purchase their own home. "Owning our own business has brought so many blessings," Roger says. "Deciding to use our Academy training and take that step was one of the best decisions we've ever made."

Mercy and Alfred **YAP**

Residential Executive Training, 2006
ACE My Business Training, 2015

Learning to Wheel and Deal

TRUCKING COMPANY

Working overseas isn't unusual for a Filipino. There's even a well-known acronym—OFW, or overseas Filipino worker—that most Filipinos know. Mercy and Alfred Yap were certainly familiar with it. Alfred was an OFW, working as a second mate on an international cargo ship, while Mercy also worked as a public high school teacher to help keep the young family—the Yaps have three children—afloat.

Being separated by an ocean was tremendously difficult for Mercy and Alfred; they wanted to be together as a family, yet they also had to provide for their family. Desperate to make a change, Mercy attended the ACE Academy in 2006, ready to gain training and learn important business principles that could bring her family together more than once or twice a year.

Shortly after finishing the Academy, Mercy found the faith and courage to start her own business. Near their house was an old hardware store, which was going bankrupt because of previous mismanagement. The owners needed to sell, and despite the dubious circumstances, Mercy felt good about buying it.

Starting her own business was intimidating, of course, especially with Alfred so far away. But buoyed up by her Academy education and carefully guided and mentored by others, Mercy took a leave of absence from teaching and set out to make

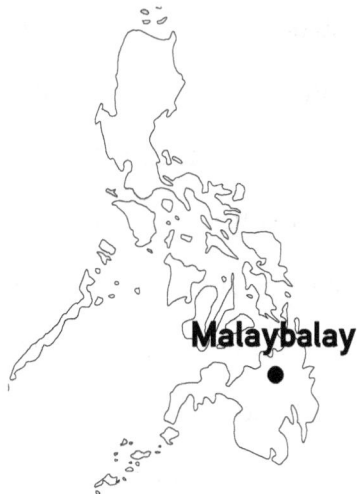

Malaybalay

"We are physically together," says Alfred. "We can spend time with our children, and although we run our businesses separately, we work together as business owners. We are complete."

her hardware store—Yap 3A Enterprises—a success.

It wasn't easy for "a woman to make it in a man's business," observes Mercy. She learned to deal with opinionated salesmen, and she personally delivered hardware supplies to her customers, once getting robbed at gunpoint. But she persevered, and Yap 3A Enterprises has consistently grown and expanded over the past decade, even extending to construction projects. Through the years, Mercy has trained her employees and created a system for the business to operate smoothly, even when she's not physically present.

Longing to be with his family, Alfred watched his wife's success from overseas—and then decided that if she could run her own business, maybe he could too. So he headed home to try his hand at being a business owner.

Alfred came from a family of truckers, so that

seemed like a logical business for him to pursue. He began with only one truck and one client, delivering diapers for a local diaper company. However, as word spread about his new venture, he picked up enough new clients that he had to buy a new truck and hire another driver.

This trend continued. By the time he bought his third truck, he had applied to be part of FastCargo Logistics, and today he owns more than a dozen 10-wheeler wing van trucks and provides delivery services throughout all of Mindanao, with a client list that includes Nestle, Del Monte, and Unilab Medicines.

The Yaps' journey toward success hasn't been easy. Giving up stable, secure employment to enter the world of entrepreneurship was daunting. They faced new challenges and tackled situations that were un-

Favorite Rules of Thumb

- Practice Kaizen
- Keep Good Records
- Hire Slow, Fire Fast
- Don't Eat Your Inventory
- Pay Yourself a Livable Salary

familiar. They had to find capital, manage accounts payable and receivable, handle employees, and plan for the future. Their Academy training—they went through the ACE My Business Program together in 2015—proved invaluable to their success as they learned to delegate and to follow rules of thumb such as **Keep Good Records**, **Hire Slow and Fire Fast**, **Don't Eat Your Inventory**, and **Pay Yourself a Livable Salary**. The mentoring they have continued to receive by actively participating in their local Academy chapter, which meets monthly, allows them to constantly improve and grow as business owners.

And above all, the Yaps are making this journey to-

gether, which is what they'd been working toward from the beginning. "We are physically together," says Alfred. "We can spend time with our children, and although we run our businesses separately, we work together as business owners. We are complete."

Kenny **LAROSA**

Residential Training, 2007
ACE My Business Training, 2018

A Celestial Solution

FUNERAL SERVICES

Owning a funeral home might not top most people's list of career goals, but for Kenny Larosa, the decision was a no-brainer. He'd been around the funeral business since he was a young boy and his mother was branch manager for a memorial and life insurance company. That company, however, didn't offer full funeral services, and Kenny's mother saw an opportunity. Partnering with an insurance company, she opened her own funeral home in 2005 that offered everything from insurance to pickup, embalming, and funeral services.

The idea was a good one, but she struggled to make it profitable. Kenny worked alongside his mom and saw that the business was floundering. Recognizing the need to gain valuable business training and skills, he signed up to attend the ACE Academy. After completing the program, Kenny decided to work abroad and earn some much-needed capital that could be put back in the company. He found a job in Abu Dhabi as an archive clerk and then in Qatar as a computer operator, while his mom kept plugging away at home.

Finally, after almost two years abroad, Kenny returned

Toledo

"This has become more than a business—it is a service we provide, one that is fast, efficient, and done with respect and dignity."

home, determined to invest both the money he'd earned and his own time and resources into building Celestial Funeral Homes into the enterprise he knew it could be.

Coming home to Toledo was not easy for Kenny; the demands of saving a failing business weighed heavily on him. But he knew if he followed the training he'd received at the Academy, he could succeed—and he also genuinely enjoyed being involved in a business that helped others and lifted their burdens during what is often a terribly difficult time.

Relying on his Academy training, Kenny created a flexible business model that allowed him to delegate specific responsibilities to skilled personnel while maintaining other responsibilities himself. For example, while Kenny is a trained embalmer, he recognized the importance of focusing his time on money management and customer service. Consequently, he now has an official embalmer, along with two assistants. In addition, his wife, Lorena, and his mother manage the office and handle the paperwork.

At the Academy, Kenny learned to recognize and respect where money comes from, so while he oversees the entire business, he focuses his time and attention on customers. He works closely with local hospitals and police stations, so he can be there quickly when his services are necessary.

"It's not easy to see so much pain," Kenny acknowledges, "but it has taught me to appreciate life more. And we recognize that in a business like a funeral home, so much respect and care is needed when we are interacting with our customers. Obviously, when someone calls us, there is a lot of emotion involved."

Integrity has become Kenny's trademark. "The

Favorite Rules of Thumb

- Integrity before Profit
- Value Your Customers
- Delay Gratification
- Practice Kaizen

aim of Celestial Funeral Homes is to give a deceased loved one the best burial possible," Kenny explains. "When we can do that, it makes letting go a little bit easier for the grieving family. This has become more than a business—it is a service we provide, one that is fast, efficient, and done with respect and dignity."

That focus has paid off, as Celestial Funeral Homes has expanded to include a memorial chapel and holds approximately 22 services a month. Even more importantly to Kenny, his company has gained a reputation for compassionate care and ethical service that make grief easier to bear.

Jimmy and Clemencia **ABALOS**

Residential Executive Training, 2004
Applied Entrepreneurship Training, 2010
ACE My Business Training, 2015

Security by the Hundreds

SECURITY GUARD TEMP SERVICES

Integrity before Profits. It sounds simple, but Jimmy and Clemencia Abalos would never have achieved success without learning how to follow this transforming business principle during their participation in the Academy.

Lingay-

The business education and training the Abaloses received at the Academy proved crucial to growing businesses they had actually started years earlier. Because these businesses are in the service sector (janitorial and security services), providing superior-quality service combined with honesty became the way they set themselves apart from their competition and ensured profit. And profit, of course, is what a business owner is working for.

Jimmy didn't start out planning to run his own business. He was 16 years old when he got his first job as a janitor at a medical center. After working for a year, he was thrilled with the chance to become custodian at a Church institute facility in Dagupan, where he worked until he left to serve a mission. After returning from his mission, he decided to change career courses, taking a job as a salesman for a gas cylinder company.

While doing that, he also found himself back at the institute building he'd been cleaning before his mission—only this time he wasn't getting paid. Instead, he volunteered to help the facilities manager with odd jobs and whatever else he needed. He worked alongside the manager, learning painting and carpentry skills. In 1990, after an earthquake hit the area, Jimmy was the natural choice to become a project supervisor, overseeing necessary repairs that needed to be made on chapels in the area.

And that's how Jimmy's career as a janitor—and the creation of his own business, JT Abalos Janitorial Service—began. "When I started this business in 1994, it was a one-man show," says Jimmy, who acknowledges that juggling being an owner, manager, and technician all in one was a challenge.

During the first few years, Clemencia helped out where she could, doing payroll and keeping records. But her full-time job as a clerk at Pangasinan State University

Favorite Rules of Thumb

- Integrity before Profits
- Keep Good Records
- Have Written Agreements

"Instead of limited income, we enjoy limitless income, and instead of being recipients of help, we are now givers of help."

kept her plenty busy. In 1999, however, she quit her job to care for the couple's one-year-old daughter, Angelica, who had been diagnosed with cancer. Thankfully, Angelica survived the cancer, thanks in large part to Clemencia's careful daily care.

In 2004, Clemencia attended the Academy's eight-week Residential Executive Program and, after finishing the course, joined Jimmy in the family's janitorial business. She was right by his side when, in 2007, he started a second company, Ensign Security Agency, which would later become Banner Security Agency.

Like his janitorial company, this second business venture was a natural extension of skills and abilities Jimmy had learned along his life's journey. While he had been working full-time to build his janitorial service, he'd also been working at his brother's security agency. Once again, Jimmy gained valuable skills by learning on the job, manning the office, and selling the services to potential clients. And once again, his expertise led him to launch a business.

The office for both businesses is located in the Abaloses' family home. Employees sit behind desks on one side of the room, answering phones and assisting clients who visit in person. On the other side is a single large piece of furniture where the magic happens: Jimmy and Clemencia's shared desk. Security caps, vests, and batons sit on a shelf in the corner. The couple work together to implement Academy rules of thumb that have brought them success and security they only dreamed of.

"Because of our business, we have switched from an

employee mindset to an employer mindset," says Jimmy. "Instead of limited income, we enjoy limitless income, and instead of being recipients of help, we are now givers of help. When poverty stopped existing for us, we were able to help people by teaching them the self-reliance skills we had learned at the Academy and encouraging them to start their own businesses."

Growing their businesses to where they are today was a Herculean journey. With the nature of their businesses, keeping up with records required to comply with government requirements is itself a test of patience and endurance. Add to that the paperwork necessary to hire, train,

schedule, and pay the more than 175 janitorial and security employees that the two companies now employ, and you can see why the Academy training became so invaluable to the Abaloses.

Clemencia shared with Jimmy all she had learned in the residential program. When he attended the Onsite Training Program six years later, he did the same. The secret to their endurance and success is that they have identified a few essential rules of thumb to follow religiously. In addition to **Integrity before Profit**, they **Keep Good Records** and **Have Written Agreements**. Thanks to the Academy, they say, they learned how to organize and "delegate, delegate, delegate."

Starting a business takes a lot of guts, the Abaloses admit, but with the Academy training, success is based less on chance and more on making smart decisions, setting long-term goals, and executing a plan. Success and self-reliance are natural byproducts, says Jimmy, when these principles are an integral part of the way one does business.

Julie and Miles **DURANO**

Residential Executive Program, 2001

Birthing a Business

BIRTHING CENTERS

More than 2.3 million Filipinos work abroad. However, while the job opportunities are tempting, being separated from loved ones is heartbreaking. Despite this, Julie Durano, a registered nurse and certified clinical instructor, found herself seriously considering the option.

Desperate to find another way to pay her bills, Julie explored the idea of starting her own business. She attended the ACE Academy's two-month residential program in 2001. When she married two years later, she encouraged her husband to try his hand at business to augment their income. The couple rented a small spot in a local marketplace and explored the idea of retailing rice. Unfortunately, the price of rice increased and this, combined with the rent they paid for their market shop, meant that income generated from the endeavor wasn't enough. Add to this dealing with dishonest employees and an encounter with a swindler, and the young couple decided to shut down the rice-retailing venture.

Julie found herself once again reluctantly considering working overseas. She discussed the possibility with one of her co-workers, another clinical instructor who had been a mentor and friend. He discouraged the move, telling her that if she was wise,

Monkayo

> Julie could do the work she loved, help decrease deaths during childbirth, and earn a decent income—all at the same time.

she could find an opportunity closer to home. In fact, he noted, in the area where she lived—Compostella Valley in Mindanao—many women die during childbirth. As a certified midwife as well as registered nurse, Julie could use her nursing education and expertise to start a birthing clinic, he suggested. Julie could do the work she loved, help decrease deaths during childbirth, and earn a decent income—all at the same time. Definitely a win-win.

With her Academy training, Julie recognized a great business opportunity when she heard it. In 2004, she quit her job as a clinical instructor and invested her entire savings to start 24-7 Family Care and Maternity Clinic, her own birthing clinic.

The road to success was rough. As a private clinic, 24-7 Family Care and Maternity didn't originally accept PhilHealth Insurance, the country's universal health coverage. That automatically eliminated many potential patients who couldn't afford help during the birthing process without insurance. In addition, Julie struggled to find staff members who could provide optimal service.

But Julie persevered. She knew that her clinic offered life-changing and life-saving services, and she was determined to succeed.

Turning to her favorite Academy rule of thumb—**Practice Kaizen**—she committed to constant improvement for herself, her staff, and her clinic. She developed a training program that improved the staff's ability not only to deliver a baby properly but also to treat patients with the best care possible throughout their time at the clinic. In addition, she searched for better ways to identify and reach out to patients who the clinic could best serve. She then focused on delivering a marketing message that emphasized the high quality of the clinic's service, as well as the equipment they offered that can assist in the birthing process.

Favorite Rules of Thumb

- Practice Kaizen
- Start Small, Think Big
- Value Your Customers

"In addition, our services are offered in a private birthing clinic, which is typically just better when compared to public facilities," Julie observes. "We offer a safe, clean environment catered to making the birthing process go as smoothly as possible."

By 2006, as more deliveries were being done in her clinic, she began to expand her services to include post-natal and family care for young children. "It just felt more complete to provide a place that not only offered birthing services but also provided proper medical care for babies," she says.

Personally, Julie also sets an ideal example of improvement and development. She loves refreshing the Academy training she received from her days in the residential program in 2001 and attends continuing ACE trainings, learning and implementing new methods for marketing and business training; her husband, Ramel "Miles," is also active in their Academy chapter.

Today, 24-7 Family Care and Maternity Clinic has grown to three branches, and Julie anticipates continued growth as clinic patient load increases. Clinic employees include midwife nurses who specialize in delivering babies and caring for pregnant women, front desk staff, and an accountant.

Julie encourages everyone who is interested in starting a business to attend the Academy. "Watching a baby being born is a magical experience," she says. "And thanks to the Academy, I am involved in that process all day, as well as watching a strong family business being born. I'm making a difference in healthy childbirth, providing quality care, and running my own business. Attending the Academy was definitely a win-win."

Job B. **FERNANDEZ**

Onsite Training, 2013

Living the "Goodlife"

FUNERAL SERVICES

After eighteen years of working for St. Peter's Life Insurance and Memorial Services, Job B. Fernandez retired. But he wasn't done working.

Job had decided to open his own memorial chapel. So, two years after retiring, Job opened a memorial services chapel—but that was just one of the companies he would eventually start. Relying on the sound business principles he learned at the ACE Academy, Job recognizes a good opportunity when he sees it, and he has since added a life-insurance company and a casket-building company to his business ventures.

Job began his adventure in the business world by partnering with three people and investing ₱3,000 from his father's business to expand and renovate a memorial chapel and start up Goodlife Memorial Chapel Company. His goal from the outset was to offer services that are both accessible and comforting during what can be an extremely difficult and painful time. With that in mind, a few months later, Job also started Goodlife Damayan Insurance Agency Company, recognizing that providing memorial services and life insurance in one place created a convenient, more affordable option for people; aside from offering life insurance, GoodLife

"Seek the kingdom of God first, and the blessings will follow. And I have definitely been blessed."

Damayan also offers a complete insurance package for the funeral.

A savvy business owner, thanks at least in part to his Academy training, Job knew a key to his success was building a strong, enthusiastic sales force for the insurance piece of the business. Insurance sales provided revenue for the memorial services company to operate, especially in the early days of the venture.

Job and his team came up with a creative way to bolster insurance sales: they launched the Kaagapay Program, which consists of a one-time payment for members who sign up. As part of the program, members receive a 30-percent discount on memorial insurance when the service is conducted in the Goodlife Memorial Chapel. To increase sales, they invited hospital and CSI personnel to be part of their selling program.

But that wasn't the only opportunity Job identified. As the Goodlife companies grew, the memorial chapel was conducting 50 to 60 funerals a month, and ordering caskets was a major expense. The next step seemed obvious to Job: cutting costs by building their own caskets.

After finding a reliable supplier of wood, Job opened a casket manufacturing facility in 2018, which not only supplies caskets for Goodlife but also offers caskets to other memorial chapels and funeral providers.

And that's not the only growth the company has seen. GoodLife Damayan opened up a second branch in Sorsogon, and Job has plans to expand into Cebu. He has also built additional memorial chapels, and he plans on adding one chapel a year for the foreseeable future.

Job looks back with gratitude to the training he received in the Academy. While attending the Onsite Training Program in his area, he was deeply inspired by the success stories of alumni that were recorded in one of the class manuals.

Favorite Rules of Thumb

- Inspect More, Assume Less
- Value Your Customers
- Pay Yourself a Livable Salary

Job kept the manual and still reads those stories often to remind himself what he is working for.

Some of his favorite Academy rules of thumb include **Inspect More, Assume Less**; **Value Your Customers**; and **Pay Yourself a Livable Salary**. Systems creation is an ongoing process for Job and his businesses; he recently hired an IT employee who helped create a system for Job's growing group of businesses.

Being an entrepreneur gives Job control over his own time, and he loves being involved in his community. Aside from serving in the Church, he is part of an interfaith group in Davao del Sur. This involvement allows him to work with others of different faiths and develop relationships of trust. He also serves as the chairman of Capitol Chaplaincy and acts as the spiritual advisor to political leaders, including the governor of Davao del Sur province, and other government employees on spiritual and moral matters. In addition, his business provides jobs for more than 50 people in his community.

Besides the time flexibility, Job is grateful for the financial security his businesses have provided. He is not only able to provide well for his family, but he has also financed some local students in their college studies.

Throughout his journey toward self-reliance, Job has always believed that obedience is key. He credits acknowledging the power of heaven and seeking divine help as the secrets to his success, along with following wise business and financial practices. "The scriptures give us the direction," he says. "Seek the kingdom of God first, and the blessings will follow. And I have definitely been blessed."

Ed and Gina **FELICIANO**

Residential Executive Training, 2009

"The Light Switched On"

ELECTRICAL CONTRACTOR

Failing in business was not where Ed and Gina Feliciano expected to be. Enthusiastic and optimistic, they had opened their own business in 2005. While they made the move out of necessity—Ed had lost his job and was barely making ends meet as a freelance electrical engineer—

they felt confident they could make it work. However, as a result of dishonest decisions made by one of their contracted workers, they were facing bad debts and suppliers clamoring for payments.

"That's not the way it was supposed to happen," says Ed.

He and Gina had started their electrical services company—now known as GINED Building Solutions Incorporated—with big dreams and tiny resources. An old table, an old phone, and a used computer, along with 3,000 pesos in their pockets, were the sum total of their assets when they opened their doors. With limited capital and few clients, they had a hard time paying their workers.

"Since we were a new company, few suppliers would trust us with credit terms, so cash was really on the short end," explains Ed, who notes that things got even more difficult after one of their workers was involved in fraudulent behavior. "I had to face my suppliers and explain to them why we couldn't pay them

Novaliches

on time. But I promised them that I would pay them, even if it took me years to do so."

While Ed was able to convince their suppliers to give him extra time, the problems didn't disappear. After running the business for several years, Ed and Gina were at their wits' end trying to make their company profitable. Their lack of business experience was evident as they experienced subpar customer and after-sales service, deals made with no clear contracts, and poor management. Ed knew something had to change, but the only solution he could see was lowering operational costs so they could eke out a meager profit month after month.

"My whole focus was on how to lower our expenses,

and it was a losing strategy because we had already lowered those costs as much as possible," he says. "There was simply no way we could reduce costs any more.

"Just when I thought the business was going under, I learned about the business course offered by the Academy for Creating Enterprise," Ed continues. "I told my wife we had nothing to lose, so we decided to check it out."

It was in the ACE business course that Ed learned a business principle that would completely revolutionize the way he looked at the business. "I heard a different tune while attending this class," he explains. "Instead of lowering expenses, I was taught to increase sales. I nev-

"We often look for worthwhile organizations where we can donate to help struggling entrepreneurs and individuals stand on their feet."

er heard that lesson as clearly as I did one day in class. The light switched on, and I said to myself, 'This is what would make my business grow.'"

From that day on, Ed and Gina did as the Academy taught, divvying up business responsibilities, with each one focusing on what they did best. Ed was a problem solver who remained calm even in stressful times while Gina had a knack for attention to details. So Ed concentrated on finding more clients and ensuring consistent sales, while Gina managed the operational side. "It was a pivotal moment in our business," Gina observes. "From then on, we found a sufficient number of clients to not only to sustain our operation but to also see growth and a healthy profit."

All the failures they had experienced during the early years of being business owners became stepping stones that they built on to achieve success. Lovers of learning, they attended seminars and workshops to bring themselves up-to-date with the latest industry practices. They read books and reference materials to keep themselves inspired and motivated to always do their best in their endeavors. And Ed continues his ACE education, attending many business seminars sponsored by the Academy, as well as monthly Academy chapter meetings.

As the company grew, the Felicianos found themselves often referring back to the simple rules of thumb they learned in the Academy, including **Start Small**, **Think Big** and **Use Multiple Suppliers**. The rule that is closest to this couple's heart, however, is **Integrity before Profit**. "Thanks to ACE, after several years I was able to go back to those suppliers that I owed money to," Ed recalls. "I was teary eyed when I finally got to pay them in full.

"Our word is our bond," Ed continues. "I don't compromise safety with lower price even if the client asks for it. I don't

Favorite Rules of Thumb

- Integrity before Profit
- Start Small, Think Big
- Use Multiple Suppliers
- Increase Sales, Decrease Costs

compete with my competitors. Rather I provide value to my service offering, and I make sure my customers understand that principle very well."

When sales had stabilized and were no longer a problem, the couple's Academy training pointed them in the direction where they should focus next: systems creation, which would deeply impact the way they ran their business. "Systems creation helped us evaluate and solve collection problems, employee challenges, and even after-sales support," Gina says. "And all the while, the success that we experienced did not blind us from fulfilling our core value: to be of help to others.

"We feel that we need to give back after being so blessed," she continues, "so we often look for worthwhile orga-

nizations where we can donate to help struggling entrepreneurs and individuals stand on their feet. We also employ young people who are preparing to serve missions and even newly returned missionaries who are still adjusting while figuring out what they are truly passionate about."

As they learned how to grow their business properly, Ed and Gina grew closer together as well, recognizing the value of spending time with each other as well as their two children, who are now grown. Through the years, they have worked to ensure that their children also understand the value of hard work, honesty, and humor—even when times get tough.

Now with 52 full-time employees, GINED offers electrical services to several large companies, including the British Embassy, Daikin Incorporated, and The Church of Jesus Christ of Latter-day Saints. Ed and Gina look at what they have achieved with amazement and gratitude. From the 3,000-peso initial capital they invested in this business, they now run a multimillion-peso company and are constantly evaluating opportunities to learn and grow in new directions.

"If anyone is looking for words of advice from me, I would tell them that starting a business is exhilarating, exciting, and energizing," says Ed. "But a lot of our success has to do with our belief that if we work hard and pay the price to learn our job, there is a Father in Heaven who will provide relief and direction. Relying on our faith that He will help us see through our business problems is comforting for us because we can sleep at night knowing that He is there to help us fight our battles."

Rocel and Agustin
ALQUISALAS

Applied Entrepreneurship Training, 2014

Crabbing for a Profit

SEAFOOD PROCESSING AND EXPORT

When Rocel and Agustin Alquisalas started MJM Seafood, their own seafood-processing business, they knew they had the necessary expertise and skill set; they had both worked in a crab processing and exporting company before, Rocel in quality control and Agustin with

Kadis

the machinery. What they didn't have, however, was the training and background necessary to make the company succeed.

Thankfully, they found that at the ACE Academy. Rocel attended the Applied Entrepreneurship Program, and Agustin dropped her off at chapter meetings and waited for her in the back of the room, where he listened intently and learned right along with his wife.

One of the most important lessons the Alquisalases learned was the value of making a profit every day. The couple discovered that they needed to have enough capital to not only start their business but also to run the business day in and day out; they used their earnings from one day to buy the next day's supplies and pay their employees. "It can be tricky when money comes in more slowly than it goes out," says Rocel, "but we applied the Academy rules of thumb and found ways to cut down on costs."

The liquefied petroleum gas they were using to cook their seafood was expensive, so they opted to use charcoal because it was a cheaper alternative. Ice for keeping their inventory cool was also quite expensive, especially because they had to buy it so frequently. Agustin solved this problem by installing three powerful air conditioners in the back of an old freight truck and creating his own cooling machine. This cooling system proved to be a lot cheaper than buying ice to keep the crab meat cool.

Rocel points out other ACE training and rules of thumb that contributed to the growth and success of MJM Seafood, including **Delayed Gratification** and **Pay Yourself a Livable Salary**. She also knows the importance of **Hiring Slow, Firing Fast**. When hiring, Rocel has learned to evaluate a potential employee's work ethic and general

Favorite Rules of Thumb

- Make a Profit Every Day
- Pay Yourself a Livable Salary
- Hire Slow, Fire Fast
- Delayed Gratification

aptitude. When she finds a person who is teachable and humble, she knows that is a good employee. "When I interview, I am most interested in a person's attitude," she explains. "Skills can be taught; work ethic cannot." Rocel has also created a system where employees rotate throughout the processing facility, cross-training on all jobs instead of learning only one.

The Alquisalases believe that the journey to owning their business was guided by God. The couple had worked for years in a crab processing and exporting company but lost their jobs several times when their contracts ended or

when the company faced financial difficulties and had to lay off employees. Rocel transferred twice to Cebu to work because of these contract problems. In addition to the inconsistent employment, the couple worried about having enough money to send their three children to college and wanted to be able to spend more time together as a family.

With these thoughts in mind, the pair sought a priesthood blessing from a beloved priesthood holder in their ward. In the blessings, they were promised success in their business as they followed the Lord. Holding fast to this promise, the Alquisalases eagerly magnify their callings in the Church, and they are dedicated to sharing what they have learned with others.

Because of their background in the crab-processing industry, as they contemplated various business opportunities, they came up with the idea of buying crabs from one vendor contact and then paying a second vendor to process the meat. They knew that if they could export quality crab meat at international prices, they would have a successful business that would provide for their needs.

> They enjoy boosting the crab-farm enterprise in their area, providing crab fishers an avenue to sell their catch daily for a solid cash profit.

They knew that having their own seafood-processing facility was an important component of this plan. Initially, they built a makeshift processing facility in the basement of their home, and within two months they were in full operation, delivering 50 kilos of crab meat at a time and keeping 10 employees busy.

The success that MJM Seafood is experiencing has blessed the Alquisalases beyond anything they could have ever imagined. Today they run their own processing facility, and they sell their product locally as well as exporting it internationally at good rates. They enjoy boosting the crab farm enterprise in their area, providing crab fishers an avenue to sell their catch daily for a solid cash profit. And all three Alquisalas children have graduated from college.

Rocel and Agustin aren't done growing by any means. The successful business couple has invested in properties, including a seaside resort property that they plan to convert into a seafood restaurant. They are also eyeing different ways to enlarge their local and international seafood export opportunities.

"One of the biggest benefits from attending the Academy is that we no longer have to scramble for work," Rocel says. "It's scary to not have a job, while being financially stable and owning our own time provides great security. Plus, being able to help others break the cycle of poverty by providing employment is truly rewarding."

Elmer B. **OWAYAS**

Applied Entrepreneurship Training, 2012
ACE My Business Training, 2017

"Nothing Less Than My Best"

REFRIGERATION AND AIR CONDITIONING SERVICES

An old toolbox and a beat-up bicycle didn't bode well for the future of Elmer B. Owayas's refrigeration and air-conditioning service. But the entrepreneur-at-heart felt hopeful, so he quit his job at an air-conditioning shop and struck out on his own, calling the humble venture Lance Refrigeration and Air Conditioning Services.

Elmer initially started in 2002 by biking from house to house, offering to repair people's air conditioning or refrigerators. Knocking on doors felt a lot like missionary work, says Elmer, who had served in the Philippines Manila Mission. His promise to always provide his clients with his best work also felt much like being on a mission, and thanks to his mantra—"Nothing less than my best"— the young businessman quickly built up a loyal clientele based on repeat customers and plenty of referrals.

Elmer's success didn't come without hard work, however. Without even knowing it, he was following a basic ACE Academy rule of thumb: **Focus, Focus, Focus**. As Elmer went from door to door, he refused to give up, focusing on one door at a time. He knew he had the technical experience necessary to succeed. After all, he'd taken

Iligan

> As Elmer went from door to door, he refused to give up, focusing on one door at a time.

a one-year vocational course and had chalked up plenty of experience repairing air conditioning and refrigerators, including two apprenticeships, one before and one after his mission.

That experience, along with tremendous patience and a passion for what he was doing, paid off as Lance Refrigeration and Air Conditioning Services (named after his oldest son, Lance) began to grow. Within a few months, Elmer had traded in his bicycle for a motorcycle, and then a multicab, allowing him to reach more potential clients. Following on the footsteps of that success, he then opened his own service center.

Within a year of hopping on his bike for the first time to sell his services, Elmer had filed for an official business permit and was providing air-conditioning and refrigeration repair services to several large corporations throughout his home town of Iligan City. He had even hired and begun training his own employees, who learned not only how to repair and service air conditioners but also to do their best, not just at work but in all aspects of their lives.

Of course, Elmer continued to learn as well. He attended the ACE Academy in 2012, where his single-minded focus was one of the institution's basic business principles. Along with that rule of thumb, Elmer notes that learning how to stay motivated and developing an entrepreneurial mindset are some of the most valuable lessons he took away from his Academy training. "It was at the Academy that I learned business management," he says, "and that capital shouldn't be a hindrance to starting a business. Rather, resourcefulness is the key."

Elmer has certainly been resourceful as he has grown Lance Refrigeration and Air Conditioning Services. He turned a toolbox and bicycle into a repair services company with 14 employees and, most recently, a Daiken distribution partner; he also add-

Favorite Rules of Thumb

- Start Small, Think Big
- Practice Kaizen
- Focus, Focus, Focus
- Value Your Customers

ed air-conditioning installation to the list of services available through his company.

However, today Elmer is much more than simply a successful entrepreneur. He is an innovator, constantly looking for ways to upgrade the quality of his services and ensuring his place as a preferred provider. He is a networker, constantly making connections with customers and refrigeration and air-conditioning companies, as well as becoming a dealer for them. And he is a bright beacon, consistently helping his own employees not just perform well in the workplace but also reach beyond that, mentoring them in the ways of entrepreneurship and self-reliance.

Somehow, the young returned missionary turned entrepreneur sensed when he hopped on his bicycle so many years ago that he and his toolbox were destined for more than just door-to-door repair work.

Rhandy B. **CONCEPCION**

Applied Entrepreneurship Training, 2016

From One Student to 700

SCHOOL AND CURRICULUM PUBLISHING

When the R. Concepcion Montessori School began operation in 2010, it was one-of-a-kind for the area. In addition to teaching by the Montessori method (blended with traditional teaching processes), it was an English-only campus, contained a speech lab, was fully air conditioned, and had a radio-frequency identification system that alerted parents when children were on campus, plus loaded money onto students' IDs for purchasing food in the cafeteria.

Despite these groundbreaking features, the school originally floundered.

The school's founder, Rhandy B. Conception, a teacher from Calaca, Batangas, describes himself as "a crazy man who has big dreams." Passionate about teaching and learning, he participated in the ACE Academy four years after starting R. Concepcion, and his experience at the Academy was key in the school's growth and eventual success. At the Academy, Rhandy identified areas to improve in and learned how to better harness the power of marketing, keep better records, and improve financial management systems. "It was at the Academy that I learned how to be a keen observer and then act on what I observed," he says.

Nasugbo

Rhandy wasn't new to education. He had taught high school

> He came up with the idea of building his own school—and the dreamer in him wanted it to be unlike any other school available in the area.

for years at St. Jerome International School and then the Philadelphia Montessori School, where he became school principal after only a year and a half. While teaching at St. Jerome, he came up with the idea of building his own school—and the dreamer in him wanted it to be unlike any other school available in the area.

Although Rhandy had no capital, he did have the skills, desire, and confidence. So he set out to turn his dream into reality. He raised money, talked up the school to almost everyone he met, and built connections. The day the school opened its doors was one of the proudest days of his life.

Initially Rhandy started small; its first year, the school had 128 students attending a pre-elementary class and grades 1 to 3. He planned on adding more buildings and grades, eventually offering a full K–12 curriculum, but that growth would be dependent on the school's success.

Rhandy anticipated challenges when the school opened

its doors. Most schools in the area were Catholic, so parents balked at the idea of a non-Catholic facility. Few schools followed the Montessori teaching method, which advocates a more hands-on approach to learning. And the school used up-to-the-date technology and offered progressive classes and programs. Rhandy's innovative approach to education was new, and people are sometimes reluctant to embrace change.

But Rhandy was persistent, and he trusted in the Lord. "I always told myself, 'Make God your business partner, and you will succeed,'" he says. That persistence paid off. The students at the school began producing some of the highest scores in their area, and the parents of the pupils were impressed by the growth of their children as well as the values they saw being taught.

Enrollment grew. With the growing number of students came more income, and more income

Favorite Rules of Thumb

- Start Small, Think Big
- Practice Separate Entities
- Integrity before Profit

meant funds for additional buildings and facilities. Rhandy continued to pursue his dream, building additional structures and adding grades as the school's finances allowed it. As the school grew, so did its reputation. Concepcion students won academic and athletic contests and achieved in regional sports and mathematics competitions. They also won a municipality Children's Congress, with one student winning the speaking category.

Today, more than 700 students attend two branches of the R. Concepcion Montessori School, which offers all the elementary and secondary education levels, including a senior high program. Rhandy is planning to open a third branch, and his long-term goal is to open up a university.

And that's not all. In 2016, Rhandy expanded the school's capability to include a publishing company— Gold Plates Publishing—where the school's textbooks are published. To date, the publishing company has published 18 pre-elementary books and more than 30 elementary books. Rhandy even published a book on the Philippines' national hero, Jose Rizal.

This innovator with big dreams has made these dreams

come true. He oversees the school he's always longed to build, where his own children proudly study. He enjoys the financial independence that comes from running his own successful business ventures. And he does it all by following his passion for educating and helping children.

Paul Ryan Erwin **GUSAY**

Residential Executive Training, 2000

The Zigzag Journey
of Paul Gusay

TRANSPORTATION/TRUCKING COMPANY

Attending the ACE Academy training felt like the perfect way to kick off a new century for Paul Gusay.

When he attended the Academy's residential program in 2000, Paul had a desire to build his own business, but he knew desire wasn't enough. "You need to have a plan and know how to implement it," he says. "That's what I was hoping to find at ACE."

And he did. At the Academy, the fledgling entrepreneur learned exactly what he needed to do to oversee his future business, including **Practice Separate Entities**, **Pay Yourself a Livable Salary**, and **Buy on Credit, Sell for Cash**.

"Cash is king," he says. "And among so many valuable lessons and principles, the Academy taught me to save business funds and put them aside solely for company use."

Armed with a solid business background, Paul now felt ready to start his own venture. However, it would take him a few years before he landed on the right business plan. After a stint working in the pharmaceutical industry, he started a trucking and supply business in 2004. Within weeks, he signed a con-

Cagayan de Oro

"Being my own boss allows me to spend more time with my family and be more involved in the education and upbringing of my children."

tract to supply vegetables to a newly opened KFC fast-food restaurant. After the successful implementation of that contract, Paul was referred to Mr. Donut, a popular donut franchise in the Philippines; he executed that contract flawlessly as well. And by 2008, Paul had ten trucks supplying and transporting for different companies.

Today, RM Viking Trade Resources Inc. transports a whole chain supply for fast-food restaurants and skillfully handles complex supply chains and logistics. And Paul's company doesn't just operate in the fast-food space. It has contracts with retail companies, grocery stores, and sanitary companies. "If you need a truck, you just have to call," says Paul, "and we'll handle the delivery for you."

Of course, the road to the company's success wasn't a straight one. "There's no direct line from point A to point B in success," Paul advises. "You have to be able to zigzag."

Much of Paul's zigzag journey to success involved implementing the principles he'd learned at the Academy, including learning to handle his customers and partners carefully and respectfully, being willing to collaborate and cooperate with others, and always doing his best, regardless of the outcome.

Owning his own business has allowed Paul to also do his best in the most important work of his life—his family. He and his wife, Liz, have four children, and Paul appreciates how the business has changed his personal life, as well as his professional life. "It has helped me become a better father," he points out. "Being my own boss allows me to spend more time with my family and be more involved in the education and upbringing of my children."

Favorite Rules of Thumb

- Practice Separate Entities
- Pay Yourself a Livable Salary
- Buy on Credit, Sell for Cash

Paul and Liz homeschool their children, and Paul is actively involved in teaching—something he can do thanks to the time flexibility that comes from being a successful entrepreneur. One of the subjects that Paul teaches is financial management. "I want my kids to develop money skills so they can be self-reliant in the future as well," he explains.

Financial security is also a huge benefit for Paul's family. Recently his youngest daughter was hospitalized, and thanks to the success of his business, he didn't have to worry about medical bills, and he was able to focus on his

child's health. "That would have been harder to do if I was an employee," he says. "I didn't have to be worried about checking in with my boss and getting time off and making up work."

Attending the Academy definitely helped Paul start the new century off right with plans for building a business that would change his life. And Paul isn't done planning. He has plans to start a social entrepreneurship company that makes homes out of eco-friendly and unique bricks that snap together, much like giant LEGO blocks. "The homes are typhoon proof," he says. "And the business would focus on empowering the impoverished. I want to help others live the kind of life I've been blessed to live."

Florido "Jun" and Bambi
TEMBLOR

Residential Executive Training, 2000 and 2001

Learning the Properties
of Success

REAL ESTATE AND PROPERTY DEVELOPMENT

Florido "Jun" Temblor Jr. doesn't have a college degree,
and when he was looking for work to support his growing
family, he was turned down over and over by employers

who wanted someone with an education. But Jun knew education wasn't the only thing that mattered, and ultimately he decided to become his own boss instead of having to work for one.

While earning a college degree wasn't possible for Jun, he knew that learning about running his own business was essential if he wanted to succeed, so he jumped at the opportunity to attend ACE Academy. That education would prove to be instrumental in the success of his business.

Making the decision to start his own business was only Jun's first step. The next step was figuring out what kind of a business he wanted to run.

As a student, Jun had bought and sold his first property. With that as a backdrop, in 2000 Jun set out create a property-for-sale website. He borrowed a camera from a friend and walked around neighborhoods, looking for people who were selling their homes. "Let me take a picture of your property," he

Dumaguete

"I was able to create my own opportunity when other opportunities were unavailable. That's what being an entrepreneur is all about."

told them, "and I'll put the photo and information about your property on my website. If you sell your house through my website, I get a commission."

Jun wasn't a professional photographer, so he spent hours studying photographs of homes on the internet to help him get an idea of what good property photos looked like. And because he didn't have reliable or fast access to the internet, he had to go to computer shops or internet cafes to upload the photos. But these were minor obstacles, and Jun was determined to succeed.

Jun called his website RealPhil.com, short for Real Estate Philippines, and it was one of the first of its kind in the Philippines. The idea was new and innovative, and initially people were slow to sign up. In addition, the time involved to list a property—contact sellers, take photos, gather information, and upload everything to the website—was lengthy. "I invested a lot of time," says Jun, whose natural persistence, hard work, and attention to detail were key to the company's success. "You certainly can't sell a property in a day."

In order to supplement his income until the business could take off, Jun also offered paid advertisements on his sites to keep the business and his family afloat while trying to sell properties.

It didn't take long, however, before people recognized the potential of Jun's business venture. Within six months, the business started to grow, even attracting buyers from other countries. As more and more people began using RealPhil.com to find quality properties in the Philippines, Jun formed other divisions within his company, including Islands Properties, which lists properties all over the Philippines, and Real Tropic Properties, which focuses on beachfront properties.

The company currently has eight employees in its main office, including several professional photographers, along

Favorite Rules of Thumb

- Start Small, Think Big
- Buy Low, Sell High
- Work on Your Business, Not Just in Your Business

with six partners located throughout the Philippines who scout for potential properties and act as a bridge between the company and buyers. Thousands of properties are listed on Jun's sites. In addition, Jun has ventured into real-estate investments and has become a successful land developer, selling both residential and business properties.

Because of the Academy, Jun was equipped with the business skills necessary to persevere through the challenges and handle the successes. Naturally reserved and quiet, Jun points to his ACE training as pivotal in helping him become more comfortable interacting with potential customers and working with others. Jun also noted that the networking opportunities were invaluable. "Having the chance to meet successful entrepreneurs and be motivated by their stories was one of my favorite parts of the Academy," he says.

His Academy education helped Jun become self-reliant, an end goal for him from the beginning. He can now comfortably provide for his family, magnify his Church calling, and serve others. One of the ways he focuses on serving is to help and influence others to become self-reliant as well. He shares his story often and has become a mentor and advisor to others who are pursuing a career in real estate.

Although Jun didn't have a college education, the Academy education he gained helped him grow and develop a business that any college graduate would be proud of. "I was able to create my own opportunity when other opportunities were unavailable," he says. "That's what being an entrepreneur is all about."

Joel **SARSABA**

Residential Executive Training, 2006

Delivering on His Vision

HARDWARE STORE

Joel Sarsaba had a vision for his life: he wanted to provide a comfortable, secure living for his family while still having flexibility and control over his own time and schedule. He knew the best way to do this was to build his own business.

What he didn't know was the best way to build that business—or even exactly what business to build.

Searching for these answers, Joel joined the ACE Academy's 54th Residential Executive Program Cebu class, a group of approximately 30 aspiring entrepreneurs who understood that with an Academy training behind them, they would know how to succeed at being a business owner.

Joel had prepared himself well for this journey. He had always wanted to go into construction because the uncle who raised him was a contractor for the Church. He had grown up around power drills and wrenches and screwdrivers, and he knew that he wanted his future to revolve around them. But tools are expensive, and Joel didn't have a lot of money.

So Joel followed an Academy rule of thumb: **Start Small, Think Big**. He identified a plan to earn the money he needed for that essential equipment.

Joel began to sell food to hungry students attending the local

> He was confident that if he did an excellent job with the clients he had, they would refer him to others, and he was right.

university. Each day he would take whatever money he had available and buy food, then he'd go on campus and sell the food at a profit. Little by little, he tucked away the funds he needed to take the next step in his business plan: buy construction tools.

Along with buying the tools, Joel made business cards to pass out to family, friends, neighbors, and fellow Church members offering home repair services such as welding, plumbing, and electrical maintenance. As those around him became familiar with his handy skills, Joel began building a reputation for himself. With each new job, Joel made sure he did a spectacular job, and this grass-roots marketing effort turned out to be immensely effective.

Joel's growing reputation for reliability caught the attention of Tony San Gabriel, president of Western Watts (now SSI), an American company founded by Ron Lindorf, an Academy supporter. Tony contracted with Joel to do one job, then another and another. It wasn't long until Joel became the regular contractor for Western Watts.

The one thing left for Joel to do in order to make his business official was to register his small company, so he needed a name. He considered names such as Common Sense or Hartley Engineering (his oldest daughter is named Hartley), but he eventually settled on Trenton Engineering, which would later be renamed Trenton Hardware and Builders when Joel opened his first hardware store.

Joel's journey to becoming a successful business owner didn't come easily. When he first started, he had no mode of transportation and few employees. Being a small name in Cebu where all the larger contracting and construction players usually landed the bigger, well-funded projects presented many challenges. But Joel remained focused on his vision.

Favorite Rules of Thumb

- Differentiate Your Business
- Start Small, Think Big
- Focus, Focus, Focus

One of Joel's favorite lessons from the Academy is to under-promise but over-deliver. He was confident that if he did an excellent job with the clients he had, they would refer him to others, and he was right. Word of mouth was—and still is—one of his most effective marketing tools. Every year he adds projects to his portfolio and pesos to his income. His excellent work and his honesty in dealing with clients have established him as a preferred contractor.

Today, Trenton Hardware and Builders has seven employees and is a reputable contracting, construction, repairs, and hardware store. In fact, in his own neighbor-

hood, Trenton's is the preferred hardware store because it is the only store in the area to offer home deliveries. This is another way Joel is following an Academy rule of thumb: **Differentiate Your Business**.

"Without the Academy, I don't know that I would have been able to turn my vision into reality," Joel says. "I wanted so much more, and the path of entrepreneurship has made it all possible."

George and Elena **LIWAGON**

Applied Entrepreneurship Training, 2012
ACE My Business Training, 2015

Tutored by Tragedy

TUTORING CENTER

Great loss can lead to great gains—sometimes in the most unexpected ways. George and Elena Liwagon and their three young children were, in their own words, "just a happy, normal family living in Davao." An engineer, George had always dreamed of owning his own construction business, and after graduating from the ACE Academy in 2012, he started GeoLenMar Manpower Services.

A teacher by profession, George's wife, Elena, specialized in math education and was head of the math department at the Precious International High School of Davao. Running her own business was far from her mind. "I'm not a risk taker," she says. "I was comfortable. We all were."

And then their nine-year-old son died from a kidney disorder. The sorrow and grief the family experienced was indescribable, and Elena particularly struggled. Trying to cope with her loss, she spent less time at home—where the pain of her missing son was so strong—and more time at work. "She was drowning herself in her job," George explains. "Yet she wasn't happy there either."

George longed to give his wife the comfort and support she so desperately needed. As he considered what he might do, he came up with a rather unique idea. Although the de-

Davao West

> At her center, she and her three tutoring employees work patiently with students of all ages, and she is even evaluating the possibility of opening a preschool.

mands of her current job were weighing heavily upon her, he knew Elena loved to teach, and he also knew she was a gifted teacher with the power to change her students' lives. So he surprised her by renting out an office space and setting up desks, chairs, and a bookshelf. Elena now had the space to start GeoLenMar Tutorial and Review Center, her own tutorial and review center.

"I was forced to retire!" recalls Elena, with a laugh.

She resigned from her position as head of the math department and started focusing on her own tutorial center. With encouragement from George, she too attended the Academy and learned what it took to run a business.

At first, she acknowledges, the principles wouldn't sink into her mind. She found them hard to grasp, and she was frustrated by business problems she was encountering for the first time. Running a business was a lot different from running a classroom. Finding pupils wasn't easy. Managing the finances was new. Marketing was foreign to her.

"I wanted to give up," Elena admits. "I wanted to close down shop and just go back to working at the school. But George said no. He wouldn't let me give up on myself."

So, following his counsel, she continued attending chapter meetings and ACE trainings and sought mentoring from the Academy's officers. And slowly but surely, her business began to grow.

The Liwagons credit that growth to careful attention to ACE rules of thumb, including ideals such as **Be Nice Later**. "It was so hard for me to be nice later," Elena says, "but I learned that it was the only way to keep the business afloat and to retain employees and clients. Being nice later doesn't mean I had to be rude and disrespectful. In fact, it had an opposite effect for me. I became more aware of my clients' needs,

Favorite Rules of Thumb

- Be Nice Later
- Differentiate Your Business
- Keep Good Records
- Value Your Customers

and I make sure my students get the best tutoring services their money could afford."

Initially, there were seven tutoring programs in the building and neighborhood where George had rented space; however, one by one, each closed their doors. Elena's Geo-LenMar Tutorial and Review Center was the last tutoring service left standing. Elena points to strong word-of-mouth marketing and repeat clients as key to her success—both of which are direct results of her Academy training.

In addition to flourishing businesses—George's compa-

ny is also going strong—the Liwagons are enjoying other benefits from their Academy participation. The time-management skills they picked up at ACE allow them to spend more time together as a family, and serving others is a priority in their lives.

In her previous position, Elena was teaching only high-school students. At her center, she and her three tutoring employees work patiently with students of all ages, and she is even evaluating the possibility of opening a pre-school—a lifelong dream. In addition, she makes her own review books for college exams and, on a daily basis, has opportunities to teach values along with mathematical principles. While the pain of losing a son will always be part of her life, Elena truly has found ways to soothe her grief by following her passion and sharing her talents to help others.

Danilo and Florence
QUINTO

Residential Executive Training, 2010
Applied Entrepreneurship Training, 2013

Finishing on a High Note

HOME FINISHING

Growing up, Danilo Quinto worked in his family's bakery, as well as their pig and poultry supply store. He cleaned up, tracked inventory, served customers, and ran the cash register. He learned early what it took to operate a family business—and he liked it. "I grew up in a business-minded and self-employed family," Danilo says. "I never really considered doing anything other than running my own business."

Discovering what that business would be took Danilo a little bit of time, however. He tried his hand at several different ventures—including selling insurance, running a printing press, and training professional boxers—before he and his wife, Florence, successfully launched 888 Home Finishing, a hardware and finishing store.

It was Florence's brother Evan who, in 2004, suggested the couple start their own tile shop. But he did more than just make the suggestion. He provided the capital for them to open a tile store and gave them their initial tiles to sell. He also set them up with a tile supplier so they could establish their own inventory.

Baguio

About the same time, the ACE Academy announced a shorter Residential Executive

> Every time a customer made a purchase at their store, the Quintos sent a handwritten thank-you note or called to leave a personal thank-you message.

Program. Previously, the Academy had offered only a two-month residential program for returned missionaries, but recognizing that many Church members couldn't be gone from family, Church callings, and work for such a long period, Academy officials designed the weeklong Residential Executive Program. A stake president at the time, Danilo was the perfect candidate. When Academy officials called and invited him and Florence to the first executive program group, they eagerly accepted.

The executive program condensed everything the regular residential program taught into a much shorter time period. The Quintos, however, still learned everything they needed to know. Specifically, the couple learned to **Use Multiple Suppliers**, compete for prices, and **Value Your Customers**. They also learned other invaluable Academy rules of thumb, including three that were particularly pertinent to them: **Buy on Credit, Sell for Cash**; **Buy Low, Sell High**; and **Start Small, Think Big**.

Thanks to the Quintos' ACE training, their business began to blossom. With no debt and outstanding credit with their suppliers, they were able to expand their stock from ceramic and granite tiles to include a wide variety of home-finishing products, including grout adhesives, laminated wood, PVC and wooden doors, electrical supplies, doorknobs, and paint.

Of course, no success comes without trials, and the growth of 888 Home Finishing was no exception. Initially, the Quintos had little to no money to invest in marketing, while their larger competitors were investing significant resources in advertising. The couple also had to work through delivery challenges and management problems.

However, their ACE training encouraged them to get creative in solving problems and

Favorite Rules of Thumb

- Buy on Credit, Sell for Cash
- Buy Low, Sell High
- Start Small, Think Big
- Value Your Customers

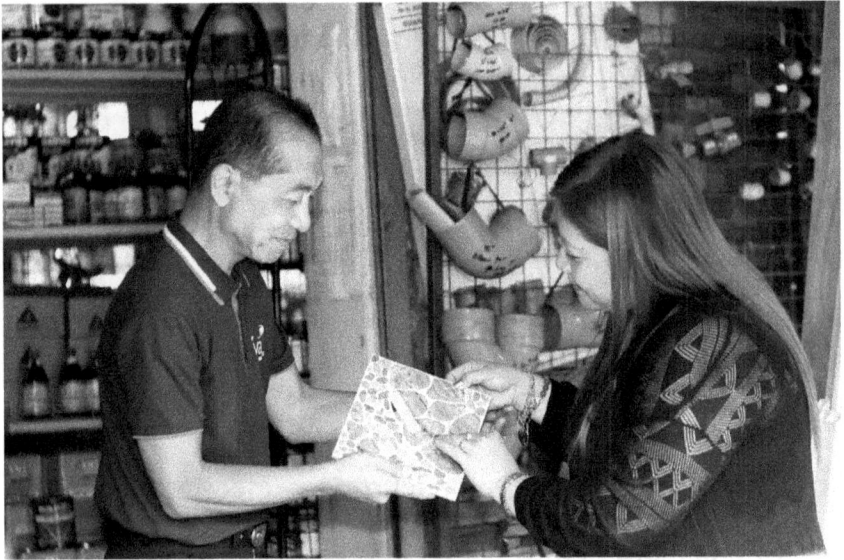

exceeding customers' expectations, so that's exactly what the Quintos did. They determined to excel at customer service, knowing that word-of-mouth advertising can be some of the most effective marketing available. "We decided if we could keep in touch with our customers, we were more likely to keep them," explains Danilo.

Every time a customer made a purchase at their store, the Quintos sent a handwritten thank-you note or called to leave a personal thank-you message. This low-cost, high-return approach made customers feel valued and built customer loyalty; the Quintos saw a lot of return customers, as well as an increasing number of referrals. They overcame other challenges by communicating better with their suppliers and employees and creating improved delivery systems and processes.

"Without challenges, life wouldn't be satisfying," Danilo declares with a chuckle, looking back at where 888 Home Finishing has come from. Looking forward is equally satisfying for the couple, who, after helping a friend build a home, decided to start their own contract and real estate development business—the perfect complement to a home-finishing business and the next step in Danilo's life of entrepreneurship.

Felix **SELMA**

Applied Entrepreneurship Training, 2011

No Longer Gripped by Fear

ADVERTISING/PRINTING SERVICES

After working for more than a decade in an advertising company, Felix Selma quit his job to manage a company for his brother-in-law. Unfortunately, that opportunity fell through, and Felix was devastated. His brother-in-law encouraged him to start his own business, but Felix had no idea where to start.

"It's not easy to start a business when you have been an employee all your life," he says. "Just thinking about it was quite overwhelming, and I was gripped with fear."

And then he heard about the ACE Academy.

Felix literally jumped out of his seat when he heard that the Academy course would be offered in his stake; he signed up immediately. "I was thinking, I have nothing to lose and everything to gain," he recalls. "I was just hoping to learn something simple from this class to help me manage this journey I was about to embark on."

Little did Felix know that the Academy would change the course of his life.

"The discussion on day one alone, Perspective and Perspective Change—I literally felt an electric energy coursing through my veins telling me that this course will be the key to my business success," he says. "The

Valenzuela

energy and confidence the Academy course gave me was so powerful. I saw exactly what I needed to do to start my own advertising business."

That was in 2011. Immediately after finishing the Academy course, Felix borrowed almost ₱3 million and started Sunbeam Advertising, a large-format printing business that makes advertising collateral and signage.

Felix started his business with only three clients, but a few years later—thanks to his excellent sales, customer service, business skills, and Academy training—he has retained those same clients and added many more. Sunbeam now has 25 employees, operates in a huge workshop in the city, and regularly manufactures and installs advertis-

ing materials for companies such as James Hardie, Green Cross, and Pioneer Adhesive, averaging approximately 100 stores per project.

"The road to where we are today wasn't easy, despite the newfound confidence I received from attending the Academy," he acknowledges. "There were many challenges along the way, including finding a location that would fit such a large operation, regular maintenance and replacement of machines and equipment, and managing employees, suppliers, and clients. I always tell myself, if there is no solution, then don't worry about it. But if there is a solution, get out there and find it."

"I always tell myself, if there is no solution, then don't worry about it. But if there is a solution, get out there and find it."

Finding solutions is part of what Felix learned at the Academy. He and his wife, Rosario, religiously check their daily operations against the rules of thumb they learned from the Academy, paying special attention to **Buy Low, Sell High**; **Buy in Bulk**; **Hire Slow, Fire Fast**; **Practice Separate Entites**, and **Pay Yourself a Livable Salary**.

"Some would think that following these simple lessons might be tedious, but for us it is one of the lifelines of the business," Felix says. Added to those time-tested and proven principles are the second-mile efforts the Selmas have incorporated into their business.

"We are committed to treating our employees right," he says. "We celebrate their birthdays in the office and do small, genuine acts that let our employees know how much their services are valued."

Finally, having a passion for what he does has been essential for Felix. "I tell people who come to me for advice to develop a passion for what they do," he says. "That passion will carry you through when struggles come your way."

Those things—sound principles, treating employees right, and feeling passion for what you're doing—have allowed Felix to build a business that has provided everything he was looking for.

Before Felix had quit his job earlier, he knew there was more. "With a salary coming in regularly, you would think we had a life that everyone dreams about, a life of security and stability," he says. "But I wanted more—I wanted more time to do what I wanted, to grow something from my passion and talents. And I wanted to spend more time with my family.

"We have learned to work together as a couple and as a company," Felix continues. "We tackle problems

Favorite Rules of Thumb

- Buy Low, Sell High
- Purchase in Bulk
- Hire Slow, Fire Fast
- Practice Separate Entities
- Pay Yourself a Livable Salary

and find solutions side by side. Growing the business has taught us to openly communicate with each other, which has strengthened our marriage. We have become stronger individually and as a family."

Felix and his family have gained much more than financial security. "The business helped us gain a better perspective about life balance," he says. "We get to assign specific time to work on our individual needs, our relationships, and our church and community responsibilities. We are able to identify and obtain focused, established, written goals. Plus this business gives us an avenue to help others."

Felix regularly hires prospective missionaries who are saving money for their missions; the company is also always open to accommodate motivated returned missionaries who need a job. "We even have a designated table for them in the office," says Felix.

Serving their own mission is hopefully on the horizon for the Selmas. Future plans include expanding operations to serve a wider range of clients and training their two sons to manage the business so they can serve short-term missions.

Felix has come a long way since those days of feeling overwhelmed and gripped with fear. But while he may have forgotten his feelings of inadequacy, he will never forget the lessons he has learned along the way. "A strong mind that continuously seeks learning, a strong will, hard work, and faith in God are key ingredients to success," he concludes.

Acknowledgments

We want to acknowledge and thank the wonderful ACE chapter leaders, now numbering more than 1,200. They volunteer their time to hold monthly meetings for nearly 6,000 Latter-day Saints, who are well on their way toward self-reliance.

We appreciate the ACE board members, several of whom have served 12 to 18 years. Special thanks to Andy Barfuss and Lew Swain, who, with the Gibsons, have been coming to board meetings for dozens of years.

We appreciate our Filipino staff, especially James and Cynthia Fantone, who have served their fellow Academy graduates as, respectively, country director and office administrator.

We thank Chris Bigelow and Kellene Adams, who have spent many hours working with Angela Fantone on the writing and producing of this, the first of hopefully many volumes of success stories profiling those who, by following the rules of thumb, have become prosperous in their lands.

Researcher and Contributor

Angela Fantone is a writer from Cebu, Philippines. True to her love of literature, she graduated with an Associate of Arts and Sciences, emphasis in English literature, from Brigham Young University–Hawaii in 2017. She has now returned to BYU–H to finish her bachelor's degree in English literature with a minor in creative writing. She has been an online English tutor and content creator, and she now works in the BYU–H writing center.

Angela began her own literary blog, *Spotlight*, where she reviews books by well-known and independent authors and promotes the arts and humanities. Her goal is to make her blog grow and gain a doctorate in creative writing so she can teach fiction writing and poetry. When not writing, she enjoys singing, cooking, and playing the guitar.